Managing Information
Second edition

David A. Wilson

**Published in association with
the Institute of Management**

Butterworth-Heinemann
Linacre House, Jordan Hill, Oxford OX2 8DP
225 Wildwood Avenue, Woburn, MA 01801-2041
A division of Reed Educational and Professional Publishing Ltd

 A member of the Reed Elsevier plc group

OXFORD   AUCKLAND   BOSTON
JOHANNESBURG   MELBOURNE   NEW DELHI

First published 1993
Reprinted 1993, 1994, 1995
Second edition 1997
Reprinted 1998 (twice), 2000

British Library Cataloguing in Publication Data
Wilson, David A., 1939–
    Managing information. – 2nd ed.
    1. Information resources management
    I. Title. II. Institute of Management
    658.4′038

ISBN 0 7506 3389 1

Typeset by Florencetype Ltd, Stoodleigh, Devon
Printed and bound in Great Britain by Biddles Ltd, *www.biddles.co.uk*

Managing Information

Titles in the Institute of Management Series

NVQ Level 3
The Competent First-Line Manager
Shields

Certificate (NVQ Level 4)
The Management Task (second edition)
Dixon

Managing Financial Resources (second edition)
Broadbent and Cullen

Managing Information (second edition)
Wilson

Managing People (second edition)
Thomson

Meeting Customer Needs (second edition)
Smith

Personal Effectiveness (second edition)
Murdock and Scutt

Diploma (NVQ Level 5)
Developing Human Resources
Thomson and Mabey

Managerial Finance
Parkinson

Managing an Effective Operation
Fowler and Graves

Managing Knowledge
Wilson

Managing in the Public Sector
Blundell and Murdock

Managing Quality
Wilson, McBride and Bell

Managing Schools
Whitaker

Managing in the Single European Market
Brown

Marketing
Lancaster and Reynolds

Tutor Support
*NVQ Handbook: practical guidelines
for providers and assessors*
Walton

Contents

Series adviser's preface

This book is one of a series designed for the people wanting to develop their capabilities as managers. You might think that there isn't anything very new in that. In one way you would be right. The fact that very many people want to learn to become better managers is not new, and for many years a wide range of approaches to such learning and development has been available. These have included courses leading to formal qualifications, organizationally-based management development programmes and a whole variety of self-study materials. A copious literature, extending from academic textbooks to sometimes idiosyncratic prescriptions from successful managers and consultants, has existed to aid – or perhaps confuse – the potential seeker after managerial truth and enlightenment.

So what is new about this series? In fact, a great deal – marking in some ways a revolution in our thinking both about the art of managing and also the process of developing managers.

Where did it all begin? Like most revolutions, although there may be a single, identifiable act that precipitated the uprising, the roots of discontent are many and long-established. The debate about the performance of British managers, the way managers are educated and trained, and the extent to which shortcomings in both these areas have contributed to our economic decline, has been running for several decades.

Until recently, this debate had been marked by periods of frenetic activity – stimulated by some report or enquiry and perhaps ending in some new initiatives or policy change – followed by relatively long periods of comparative calm. But the underlying causes for concern persisted. Basically, the majority of managers in the UK appeared to have little or no training for their role, certainly far less than their counterparts in our major competitor nations. And there was concern about the nature, style and appropriateness of the management education and training that was available.

The catalyst for this latest revolution came in late 1986 and early 1987, when three major reports reopened the whole issue. The 1987 reports were *The Making of British Managers* by John Constable and Roger McCormick, carried out for the British Institute of Management and the CBI, and *The Making of Managers* by Charles Handy, carried out for the (then) Manpower Services Commission, National Economic Development Office and British Institution of Management. The 1986 report, which often receives less recognition than it deserves as a key contribution to the recent changes, was *Management Training: context and process* by Iain Mangham and Mick Silver, carried out for the

Economic and Social Research Council and the Department of Trade and Industry.

It is not the place to review in detail what the reports said. Indeed, they and their consequences are discussed in several places in this series of books. But essentially they confirmed that:

- British managers were undertrained by comparison with their counterparts internationally.
- The majority of employers invested far too little in training and developing their managers.
- Many employers found it difficult to specify with any degree of detail just what it was that they required successful managers to be able to do.

The Constable/McCormick and Handy reports advanced various recommendations for addressing these problems, involving an expansion of management education and development, a reformed structure of qualifications and a commitment from employers to a code of practice for management development. While this analysis was not new, and had echoes of much that had been said in earlier debates, this time a few leading individuals determined that the response should be both radical and permanent. The response was coordinated by the newly-established Council for Management Education and Development (now the National Forum for Management Education and Development (NFMED)) under the energetic and visionary leadership of Bob (now Sir Bob) Reid formerly of Shell UK and the British Railways Board.

Under the umbrella of NFMED a series of employer-led working parties tackled the problem of defining what it was that managers should be able to do, and how this differed for people at different levels in their organizations; how this satisfactory ability to perform might be verified; and how an appropriate structure of management qualifications could be put in place. This work drew upon the methods used to specify vocational standards in industry and commerce, and led to the development and introduction of competence-based management standards and qualifications. In this context, competence is defined as the ability to perform the activities within an occupation or function to the standards expected in employment.

It is this competence-based approach that is new in our thinking about the manager's capabilities. It is also what is new about this series of books, in that they are designed to support both this new structure of management standards, and of development activities based on it. The series was originally commissioned to support the Institute of Management's Certificate and Diploma qualifications, which were one of the first to be based on the new standards. However, these books are equally appropriate to any university, college or indeed company course leading to a certificate in management or diploma in management studies.

The standards were specified through an extensive process of consultation with a large number of managers in organizations of many different types and sizes. They are therefore employment based and employer-supported. And they fill the gap that Mangham and Silver identified – now we do have a language to describe what it is employers want their managers to be able to do – at least in part.

If you are engaged in any form of management development leading to a certificate or diploma qualification conforming to the national management standards, then you are probably already familiar with most of the key ideas on which the standards are based. To achieve their key purpose, which is defined as achieving the organization's objectives and continuously improving its performance, managers need to perform four key roles: managing operations, managing finance, managing people and managing information. Each of these key roles has a structure of units and elements, each with associated performance and assessment criteria.

The reason for the qualification 'in part' is that organizations are different, and jobs within them are different. Thus the generic management standards probably do not cover all the management competences that you may need to possess in your job. There are almost certainly additional things, specific to your own situation in your own organization, that you need to be able to do. The standards are necessary, but almost certainly not sufficient. Only you, in discussion with your boss, will be able to decide what other capabilities you need to possess. But the standards are a place to start, a basis on which to build. Once you have demonstrated your proficiency against the standards, it will stand you in good stead as you progress through your organization, or change jobs.

So how do the new standards change the process by which you develop yourself as a manager? They change the process of development, or of gaining a management qualification, quite a lot. It is no longer a question of acquiring information and facts, perhaps by being 'taught' in some classroom environment, and then being tested to see what you can recall. It involves demonstrating, in a quite specific way, that you can do certain things to a particular standard of performance. And because of this, it puts a much greater onus on you to manage your own development, to decide how you can demonstrate any particular competence, what evidence you need to present, and how you can collect it. Of course, there will always be people to advise and guide you in this, if you need help.

But there is another dimension, and it is to this that this series of books is addressed. While the standards stress ability to perform, they do not ignore the traditional knowledge base that has been associated with 'management studies'. Rather, they set this in a different context. The standards are supported by 'underpinning knowledge and understanding' which has three components:

- Purpose and context, which is knowledge and understanding of the manager's objectives, and of the relevant organizational and environmental influences, opportunities and values.
- Principles and methods, which is knowledge and understanding of the theories, models, principles, methods and techniques that provide the basis of competent managerial performance.
- Data, which is knowledge and understanding of specific facts likely to be important to meeting the standards.

Possession of the relevant knowledge and understanding underpinning the standards is needed to support competent managerial performance as specified in the standards. It also has an important role in supporting the transferability of management capabilities. It helps to ensure that you have done more than learned 'the way we do things around here' in your own organization. It indicates a recognition of the wider things which underpin competence, and that you will be able to change jobs or organizations and still be able to perform effectively.

These books cover the knowledge and understanding underpinning the management standards, most specifically in the category of principles and methods. But their coverage is not limited to the minimum required by the standards, and extends in both depth and breadth in many areas. The authors have tried to approach these underlying principles and methods in a practical way. They use many short cases and examples which we hope will demonstrate how, in practice, the principles and methods, and knowledge of purpose and context plus data, support the ability to perform as required by the management standards. In particular we hope that this type of presentation will enable you to identify and learn from similar examples in your own managerial work.

You will already have noticed that one consequence of this new focus on the standards is that the traditional 'functional' packages of knowledge and theory do not appear. The standard textbook titles such as 'quantitative methods', 'production management', 'organizational behaviour' etc. disappear. Instead, principles and methods have been collected together in clusters that more closely match the key roles within the standards. You will also find a small degree of overlap in some of the volumes, because some principles and methods support several of the individual units within the standards. We hope you will find this useful reinforcement.

Having described the positive aspects of standards-based management development, it would be wrong to finish without a few cautionary remarks. The developments described above may seem simple, logical and uncontroversial. It did not always seem that way in the years of work which led up to the introduction of the standards. To revert to the revolution analogy, the process has been marked by ideological conflict and battles over sovereignty and territory. It has sometimes been unclear which side various parties are on

– and indeed how many sides there are! The revolution, if well advanced, is not at an end. Guerrilla warfare continues in parts of the territory.

Perhaps the best way of describing this is to say that, while competence-based standards are widely recognized as at least a major part of the answer to improving managerial performance, they are not the whole answer. There is still some debate about the way competences are defined, and whether those in the standards are the most appropriate on which to base assessment of managerial performance. There are other models of management competences than those in the standards.

There is also a danger in separating management performance into a set of discrete components. The whole is, and needs to be, more than the sum of the parts. Just like bowling an off-break in cricket, practising a golf swing or forehand drive in tennis, you have to combine all the separate movements into a smooth, flowing action. How you combine the competences, and build on them, will mark your own individual style as a manager.

We should also be careful not to see the standards as set in stone. They determine what today's managers need to be able to do. As the arena in which managers operate changes, then so will the standards. The lesson for all of us as managers is that we need to go on learning and developing, acquiring new skills or refining existing ones. Obtaining your certificate or diploma is like passing a mile post, not crossing the finishing line.

All the changes and developments of recent years have brought management qualifications, and the processes by which they are gained, much closer to your job as a manager. We hope these books support this process by providing bridges between your own experience and the underlying principles and methods which will help you to demonstrate your competence. Already, there is a lot of evidence that managers enjoy the challenge of demonstrating competence, and find immediate benefits in their jobs from the programmes based on these new-style qualifications. We hope you do too. Good luck in your career development.

Paul Jervis

Preface

Did you have a good day at the office yesterday?

As a manager there's a chance you spend at least part of your day in an office – but your day probably wasn't all good. Did you just sit at a clear desk refining your five-year strategic plan? More likely your day was a series of short-term crises – a quality problem, a customer wanting lower prices, a changed specification, someone off sick ... And now you have the niggling feeling that yesterday, yet again, you got no nearer solving the important fundamental question: how to break out of fire-fighting mode, and start managing proactively.

If it's any consolation, you are not alone: we're all sick of hearing how fast-moving and competitive business is today. Most managers are anxious about the future, and with good cause too. The relentless advance of information technology is utterly transforming jobs and whole industries – and sweeping some away entirely. Today do you know of a typewriter manufacturer? And tomorrow will bank branches be recognizable in the high street – or be there at all, for that matter?

The fate of the banking sector is a good indicator of what could well befall any other industry which handles information. Money, after all, is only a special form of information, and yet some banks see the information revolution as a threat – but others see it as an opportunity to be exploited.

For instance, most banks are competing on cost by cutting staff and using computers to automate their processes. In 1990 almost 500,000 managers and clerical staff worked in the banks, but by the year 2000, about 200,000 of these jobs will have disappeared. However, over the same period First Direct, the UK home banking company, has been taking a different approach. They started from nothing to grab half a million customers, and could well double that by the year 2000. Instead of automating to cut costs, First Direct uses computers to offer an entirely new and more attractive banking service, which just happens to be cheaper as well.

How about you? Do you see computers as a threat? If so, perhaps it is because you, like many others, have never had a chance to learn about the opportunities they can bring. Most managers admit they could not do their jobs without computers, yet many are scared of them. But before long if you don't manage information to deliver a better, cheaper product or service, again you won't be alone: you could be with 200,000 ex-employees from the banking sector.

There will never be a better time to hone your skills, and learn what's possible with the new technology. Also you might like to prove your competence by qualifying for the new competence-based Certificate or Diploma in Management being promoted by the Management Charter Initiative.

This book is written to get you started.

David A. Wilson

Free OHP slides and notes

There is a Microsoft Powerpoint presentation suitable for introducing a course on Managing Information, available free at the Butterworth-Heinemann Web site. It includes screen shots from the Internet and a variety of PC applications. This may be viewed, or downloaded by students or tutors, for adapting and printing onto overhead projection foils. The URL for the site is http://WWW.bh.com.

1 The difference information can make

Why is this chapter relevant?

The explosion of interest in the Internet, or Global Super Highway, as the popular media have dubbed it, is an example of how rapidly new information products can catch the public imagination and take off commercially. In the 1992 edition of this book the Internet was only mentioned once, almost accidentally, and the focus was on how to manage business more cheaply and more proactively by using computers.

The focus is still the same, but now with a cheap, accessible communications infrastructure in place, it feels like we're sitting on top of a volcano: there is about to be an eruption of new commercial activity which will envelop everyone at work, with unpredictable consequences. The Internet will not only bring new cheaper, more efficient ways of working, it will also bring new consumer products and services. The combined effect is that the risks and the rewards in business have just been upped. During the lifetime of this edition some people will lose their jobs to a computer, some will find their jobs utterly transformed, and a few will be catapulted into jobs of unimagined status and influence.

The rate of change in the business world as we approach the new millennium will inevitably get faster. To survive in this environment, you and your organization must learn to be flexible and responsive to your customers' needs. Knowing about computers, and using them appropriately is no longer an option. You'll be dead if you don't.

This introductory chapter sets the scene – describes the changing business environment – and shows that information and the way it is managed is the key to survival and success.

> Frowning, Jo swung round from the office desk, walked across to the percolator and poured a cup of black coffee. Through the window, clouds were building in the darkening sky above the Business Park. The office staff had gone home two hours ago, the car park was nearly empty and the street lights were beginning to come on.
>
> The aroma from the percolator evoked holiday memories – of family breakfasts in the sunshine with French bread, cherry jam and steaming hot café au lait. That seemed so long ago. The

only money problem then was finding the nearest cash dispenser – a far cry from wrestling with cash flows and profit forecasts, with no obvious escape from the relentless squeeze between low revenue and rising costs. On the personal computer screen the spreadsheet glowed brightly, with a liberal scatter of red figures along the bottom line. 'The trouble is', Jo thought, 'we've already made all the obvious cuts. All that's left are fixed costs, and if we try cutting into those, our revenue will inevitably fall too.' On impulse Jo strode across to the keyboard, increased sales prices by 25 per cent and watched black figures replace red, as the higher revenue cascaded through to a healthy balance on the bottom line.

Of course the market wouldn't bear price rises of 25 per cent. 'I'm not playing "What-if" here. I'm playing "if-only".

Gloomily, Jo took another sip of coffee.

Recognize the scenario? Perhaps you do because helping run a successful organization is difficult – and rapidly getting more difficult as markets become more competitive and consumers become more demanding.

However, there is a way out through 'better management' – which in other books might be tackled under the headings of marketing, finance or operations, but here will be explained in terms of how you and others in your organization manage information.

In the opening scenario, Jo is wrestling with poor margins coupled with inelasticity of demand – a typical problem in today's competitive markets – and yet in many markets there are players who can apparently charge a premium for their services or products. Furthermore, the basic service or product offered by these privileged players is often not very different from that offered by less successful players in the same market: the premium product often clearly requires similar inputs of direct labour and direct materials. So how is it they can charge more? It must be the way the direct labour and materials are put together. Now here's the key: the way they are put together depends upon that magic ingredient – information – which costs something to acquire, but never gets diminished however many times you draw upon it.

The value of information

When you want a sandwich for lunch, do you buy the cheap, dried-up one from the crumby tray – or given the chance would you select a more expensive creation which is carefully packed and looks fresh and appetizing? You would probably choose the more expensive

Model	Power (bhp)	Length (in.)	Width (in.)	Height (in.)	Weight (kg)	Max. speed (mph)	Accel. 0–60 (s)	Fuel cons. (mpg)	Price (£)
Ford Escort 1.4 Estate	71	181	74	55	1051	105	14.0	35.7	£11,960
Lada Riva 1.5 Estate	66	162	64	56	1020	97	14.0	32	£5,895

Figure 1.1   *Specifications and prices of Lada Riva and Ford Escort Estates* (Source: *What Car*, August 1996)

sandwich, unless you are down to your last dime – or at any rate more and more consumers would, as expectations and disposable income gradually increase.

Quality and design are clearly very important factors in determining the price which the consumer will pay for products or services. It is true for trivial items such as sandwiches and it is also true for major purchases such as cars. Compare the two specifications for five-seat smaller estate cars shown in Figure 1.1.

On the face of it these two estate cars are very similar, and yet the Ford is more than twice the price of the Lada. Even so you will probably not be surprised that in the UK the modern design, better quality Ford outsells the cheaper Lada.

So what can we learn from this example? The main lesson is that, from the customers' point of view, the Ford represents a far more attractive combination of raw materials than the Lada. In other words, starting with the same kinds of input – similar materials and probably similar amounts of direct labour – one manufacturer builds in more know-how and thereby adds more value than the other. Know-how of course includes, for example, design information, quality information and production information. Presumably the manufacturers of the Lada would like to know how to build a better car and charge more for it, and thus it seems that their problem is directly related to how they manage information.

How to manage information

All organizations must manage information, just as all businesses must make a profit, but for a chief executive to tell you to improve your information management, like telling you to improve profits, is no help at all. What you need is more specific direction on the route to those overall goals, and that is what this book aims to do.

But before we rush on too far, is it fair to elevate managing information to the same level of importance as making a profit? It could be argued that, however well you manage information, without profits your business will fail. On the other hand, without information decisions are impossible, and profitability depends upon good decision-making throughout the organization. Decision-making is central to every manager's role, and whole books have been devoted to just this subject by authors such as Herbert Simon and Peter Drucker, who belong to and have helped create the decision-making school of management thought, the importance of which is difficult to overestimate.

Decisions are impossible without information and managers are constantly seeking more and better information to support their decision-making, hence the growth of information systems – a term which today is often taken to mean networks of computers, but strictly speaking should also include non-computerized channels of communication such as regular meetings, the in- and out-trays full of memos and reports, and of course the phone. To survive, every organization must have an information system. All organizations must be able to collect information, communicate it internally and process it so that managers can make decisions quickly and effectively in pursuit of organizational objectives in a changing, competitive environment. The information system is the nervous system which allows an organization to respond to opportunities and avoid threats; to be effective it must reach into the furthest extremities of the organization.

The role of computers

Computers and electronic communications networks are destined to play an ever bigger role in the handling of information, for three reasons:

● Processing: computers are more accurate, and cheaper than people.
● Communication: electronic messaging is faster, and cheaper than paper.
● Storage: electronic files are more accessible, and cheaper than paper.

Cheap, accurate processing

In banking, for instance, computers have generated massive permanent savings by completely removing the need for large amounts of routine paperwork and the army of clerks who process it. An obvious example is the demise of the cheque book. You may have noticed that your bank statements show many more automatic entries such as card purchases, direct debits and automated cash, and rather fewer cheque entries. Not long ago thousands of millions of cheques where drawn annually in the UK. Each cheque had to be physically transported to the recipient's bank for cashing, then returned to its home bank for deducting from the drawer's account. Machines were used for automatically sorting and processing, but this could only be done after each individual cheque had been manually encoded to make it machine readable. Banking personnel did this using a keyboard device called a magnetic character inscriber. It cost the banks literally millions of man- and woman-hours on clearing cheques – a strong incentive for them to replace the paper-based cheque system with electronic funds transfer, wherever possible.

£4 billion – the large cost of small change

Banks plan an alternative to coins and notes

When your daughter phones late at night to say she's low on petrol and hasn't got any money, it would be really handy just to transfer £10 over the phone line from your purse into hers. Of course that's impossible right now, but not for much longer if the Mondex consortium of NatWest, Midland and other banks have their way.

Around £4 billion each year is spent on just handling and maintaining the bulky coins and notes we all carry around for casual spending. That's one reason for the Mondex smart card – a kind of purse for electronic cash (e-cash). E-cash will save money for the banks, but it will be convenient for customers too – less bulky, never requiring change, and useful for sending and receiving over the phone and Internet. E-cash cards will be much simpler to administer – no creditworthiness to check, no maintaining of card accounts and subsequent billing and receiving of payments. As with hard cash, the whole transaction is completed instantly at the point of sale.

In July 1995 a two-year Mondex pilot project was started in Swindon, and after only a year, about 20 per cent of Midland and NatWest customers in the town were using the e-cash card. When credit cards were first introduced, it took four years to reach that level of uptake. This is encouraging, but it may take a 'killer application' – a new and exciting commercial use – to boost Mondex in the same way that Visicalc, the first spreadsheet program boosted the Apple personal computer into the limelight.

If card readers become common on domestic and public phones, then sending money to your daughter could be as easy as using an ATM cash machine. With a card reader at home you'd scarcely need to visit the high street. To refill your electronic purse, you'd just phone your bank to draw e-cash from your current account and put it onto your e-cash card.

The availability of e-cash is sure to change the business environment. We can anticipate more direct line banks and fewer in the high street. Niche retail markets will be won by the Internet virtual shopping mall, at the expense of conventional retailers. Will the Internet be the killer application? If so, perhaps soon we will never again need to have the right coins for the parking meter or the bus ticket.

However, you won't be able to spin your Mondex card to see who serves first at tennis, or play shove ha'penny with it in the pub.

Cheap, fast messaging

The second reason why networks of computers are becoming widespread is their ability to speed up the whole trading cycle, resulting in more productive use of assets and faster response to customer requirements. For instance the buyers in organizations are beginning to link up their computers with those of their suppliers so they can exchange information electronically. Using Electronic Commerce, or Electronic Data Interchange (EDI) as it used to be called, the whole process of inviting tenders, receiving quotations, placing orders, receiving the invoices and paying – which took weeks using the postal service – can now be completed the same day if necessary. Electronic commerce offers lots of advantages: the money comes back to the seller more quickly, the buyer needs lower stocks to support a given level of trading, and planning is much easier for both. In fact it makes the whole process easier and, as we shall see in Chapter 6, makes it more likely that orders will go to suppliers who have EDI links with their customers.

Cheap, accessible filing

The third reason why computers are sure to take over in more and more areas of organizational life is that they can make any information already collected for one purpose instantly available to be used for many other secondary purposes. This is opening up totally new ways of using information. Let us take, for example, the way information about groceries bought by customers can be used in a retail outlet. In corner shops the till is often operated by the proprietor and once the customer has paid for his or her purchases the only record of the transactions is on the till roll – to all intents and purposes inaccessible. It is of little consequence though because the proprietor is close enough to the action for decision-making and knows roughly what the day's takings were, how many customers have been served and whether there has been a run on a particular item.

In the supermarket, however, there may be 30 checkout operators and 10,000 or more different lines stocked. At peak times items may be leaving the supermarket at a rate of 40,000 items per hour. Stocks of each line must be reordered to arrive at the rate of consumption, or changing demand for particular lines caused by promotional activity or food scares could easily lead to empty shelves or over-stocking. The supermarket therefore cannot afford to throw away till-roll data, which has been collected anyway, to work out how much to charge the customer – the primary use. Once collected it must be used again for stock control, a secondary use. And that's not the end of the story: information is expensive to collect, but once held in digital form it costs next to nothing to store and so can be freely used over and over again for a variety of secondary purposes. As a last example, till-roll data collected over a period of months or years can be analysed for long-term trends and presented graphically to aid in forecasting and strategic planning.

Information overload

At a personal level we all know that more information of every type is now available than ever before. How often nowadays are you 'personally selected' both at home and at work, for the chance of receiving a fabulous holiday – and some information? Most of it is junk information – junk mail, junk faxes and junk memos which you file straight away in the waste paper bin – and guess who personally selected you? A computer of course. Computers are great for sending out information: more computers are used for word-processing than for any other task. They are also amazingly fast at processing some types of data, in particular financial and numerical data once they have been converted into electronic digital signals, but no computer yet invented can receive an item of junk mail, read it and decide what to do with it.

So history is repeating itself: the invention of the typewriter with its high output of 30 or 40 words per minute did not lead us to employ fewer scribes to write letters and other documents. Instead we employed more people to produce much more written work, and now the word processor is having the same effect. The net result is more people with keyboard skills than ever before, and far more information on every conceivable subject, competing for our attention and, more often than not, failing to get it.

It seems that, far from solving our problems, the computers we use to help us manage information by processing data faster actually create new problems by adding to the volume, variety and complexity of information available. Nevertheless, some organizations thrive in this new environment; they use computers and modern information systems to make better decisions more quickly, allowing them to respond faster to customer requirements, which in markets today is a massive competitive advantage.

Responsiveness to customer needs

Nobody likes being kept waiting, and we are often prepared to pay to avoid it. When you get back from your holidays you can save money by posting off your holiday snaps to a cut-price processor – or you can pay a premium to have them back within the hour from Supasnaps or Boots in the high street.

Business customers don't like to be kept waiting either; it can actually cost them money, and so suppliers who deliver promptly have a significant edge on their competitors. To be able to deliver standard items fast, suppliers need only hold stocks, but for services, and products designed specially to the customer's requirements, stock holding is not possible. The ability to deliver promptly then depends upon how well the organization can marshal its resources to make and deliver to meet the customer's order. And this involves fast, efficient handling of information – about what to make and how to make it.

Mazak win markets, with factory information

Yamasaki Mazak, the Japanese machine-tool manufacturers, have a factory in Worcester, close to Coventry where British manufacturers once made and supplied machine tools around the world. However, the Mazak automated factory does not manufacture for stock, and yet can deliver to their customers' specifications within one or two months. This is amazingly fast when you consider that other manufacturers typically quote a six-month delivery. Mazak never make batches of product, as used to be the custom in Coventry. In this way they keep each of the stages in the manufacturing process free of the log-jams and queues which develop with batch production. Thus they can speed their customers' special requirements through the factory without delay. The Mazak factory produces up to 100 machines a month, in a range of 55 different models. Each model has optional features, and so the same product is seldom produced twice running. Each order requires a different set of manufacturing instructions.

How do they handle this factory information? They use CAD (computer-aided design), CAM (computer-aided manufacture) and CIM (computer-integrated manufacture). Customer orders and specifications are processed on the screens of CAD workstations. Then this design information is transferred electronically to the screen of process planners who work at CAM workstations. Here the design information is converted into CNC (computer numerical control) programs which are used to control the automatic machine-tool processes used in the factory. A paperwork system just would not be fast enough. All the computers and machine tool processes are linked up together through a computer network, and the whole production process is scheduled and co-ordinated by a supervisory computer to form an advanced example of CIM.

And what does this all mean to the customer? It means taking delivery of an individually designed, high-quality product only two months after placing the order instead of six months – bringing forward the pay-back period or break-even point by a massive four months. No wonder the Japanese dominate the world market in machine tools. Yamasaki Mazak are truly world-class performers.

World markets

Factories like the Mazak one in Worcester are not a curious phenomenon that we can afford to ignore: they represent the pattern of the future. Our cosy, protected home markets are disappearing fast, as the Americans and Japanese buy companies or build factories here. The distinction between home and export markets is disappearing, as tariffs, quotas and technical barriers to trade across Europe are removed. The world is rapidly becoming a global marketplace in which only the world-class players thrive.

This is great news for us as consumers because it means we can choose from the best value products and services available in the world. But as managers of organizations it means we face dramatically increased competition.

World-class performance

'World class' is a term used by Dick Schonberger, an American consultant and professor at the University of Washington, to describe any organization which is consistently held in the highest regard by its customers, and can therefore compete successfully in world markets. Tom Peters, another American, author of *In Search of Excellence*, *Thriving on Chaos* and *Liberation Management*, describes these organizations as 'excellent'. The important point to note, however, is that, somehow, these excellent, world-class organizations are consistently able to meet and often exceed their customers' expectations.

This kind of exceptional performance cannot happen by chance: it must be made to happen by applying a systematic approach with great dedication. Why? Because customer expectations are constantly rising. What we as consumers are delighted with today, we come to expect tomorrow, and so any organization that stands still on quality and customer service is soon left behind.

The only way to excel in world markets is through continual improvement. The Japanese word for improvement is *kaizen*, a word which they now use in a business context to describe the group of techniques used to achieve continual systematic improvement. In the West we group together the same techniques under the title of total quality management (TQM).

Total quality management

TQM is well established in the UK, promoted actively by the Department of Trade and Industry (DTI) through its 'Managing into the 90s' initiative. The DTI holds the view that the ability to believe fervently in a better future is not a uniquely Japanese characteristic. British employees – managers and workers together – are also capable of sharing a fervent belief in a better future. Under the right circumstances it can become a self-fulfilling belief, which is not dependent on a kamikaze culture but upon the human characteristics of hope, ambition, intellect and team spirit.

The DTI is using TQM as a medium for getting the message across to British organizations: the old styles of management which seemed to work at the beginning of the century, clearly don't work any longer. The old styles depended on delegation of authority and responsibility from the brainy top, down to the brawny bottom levels. Organizations in which a few managers manage, and many labourers labour, become victims of the intellectual bottleneck at the top. Too many changes are needed on too many fronts for the few at the top to take all the decisions necessary – or even to monitor them all closely.

Instead, the new styles of management recognize that workers too are – or at any rate should be – managers to some extent. Indeed the terms 'management' and 'workers' perpetuate outdated attitudes such as the 'ours is not to reason why' attitude at lower levels, and the 'you don't need to know about that' attitude at higher levels. The new successful organizations are those in which managers are coaches rather than sergeant majors, where information is more freely accessible, and where everyone makes an intellectual contribution to a better future.

It all sounds too revolutionary for some chief executives to stomach: it seems to require a supreme act of faith – to abandon the deeply held old beliefs about how managers manage, and to replace them with new radically different methods. But for those chief executives who do take the plunge, the rewards have proved staggering. For instance, in 1981 British Airways were losing on average £200 per minute, until Chief Executive Officer (CEO) Sir Colin Marshall launched 'Putting People First' – a TQM programme. Within three years BA was profitable again, and has remained so even through the Gulf crisis and the recession when other major world airlines were struggling – and some like Pan Am failing – to survive.

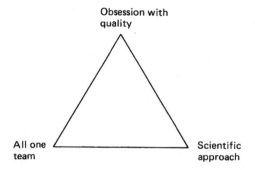

Figure 1.2 *The Joiner triangle*

So what is TQM? Organizations like to customize their TQM programmes and promote them internally under a variety of different names. But in fact 'Putting People First' at BA has much in common with 'Kaizen' at the Nissan plant in Sunderland, with 'Market Driven Quality' at IBM, with 'First Service' at W. H. Smiths, and with 'Quality, Efficiency, Service to all (QUEST)' at Oxford County Council.

All these programmes can be thought of as TQM because, to some extent, they all address the three essential requirements for continual improvement. These are neatly summarized in the Joiner triangle devised by Brian Joiner, of Joiner Associates, Wisconsin, USA, to drive home their fundamental importance (see Figure 1.2). Let us take a brief look at each of these essentials because, as we shall see, information management underpins them all.

Obsession with quality

Quality in this context does not have its usual meaning of conformance to specification. Instead, to underline the importance of the customer these days, it is defined as 'exceeding customer expectations'. This dramatic change in thinking comes as a major culture shock to organizations first exposed to TQM, and managing the change to achieve this revolution must start, as we have seen, right at the top, with the chief executive. Without total commitment from the chief executive the lengthy training programmes for spreading the TQM gospel will be just another costly burden on the organization. There are so many instances of chief executives sounding off about the importance of quality, and then compromising as soon as the pressure is on and, for instance, authorizing the shipment of a batch of questionable quality if it would otherwise miss its delivery date. Managers at every level take their lead from what the chief executive does, and they ignore the rhetoric. Actions speak louder than words, and TQM will only work when the whole organization from top to bottom is truly obsessed with quality in its newly understood sense.

Managing change of this magnitude requires information management of the highest order because of the far-reaching effects of change on the motivation and working practices of everyone in the workforce team.

All one team

The focus on the customer in TQM programmes needs explaining because another new concept is used, that of the 'internal customer'. It is used to emphasize how important it is for individuals and departments to work together as a team, rather than pursuing narrow local objectives and blaming each other or passing the buck when things go wrong. Dick Schonberger talks of building a chain of customers, where the 'customer' is defined as the person or department that receives the output of each person's or department's work, regardless of whether they are inside or outside the organization. When this can be done, the result is a workforce who pull together as a team towards overall objectives, rather than focusing on narrow departmental objectives and pulling the organization apart by competing internally.

Teamwork of course depends on good communications and the free flow of information within the organization. Communications problems are usually more severe in larger organizations, and progressive bigger companies are seeking ways to improve communications. One approach being tried by British Airways, British Petroleum and others, is to adopt new organizational structures with fewer layers in the hierarchy – the so-called 'flatter' organization. Also, many companies are investing in computer networks to provide management information, with a personal computer on every manager's desk. These are two ways of 'enabling' managers throughout the organization, by making it easier for them to get hold of the information they need to do their job, to co-operate and to pull together as a team.

Scientific approach

Can you imagine playing hunt the thimble without someone calling 'getting warmer' or 'colder'? Progress towards any goal requires change, and quick feedback to indicate whether the most recent change brought you nearer to or further from your goal. In fact the more information you have the better: it is useful to know how much nearer or further – and that requires measurement, a theme we shall return to later.

Thus to improve something at work, you must change it in some way. An improvement is simply a change for the better, and the TQM philosophy of continual improvement should encourage everyone constantly to be on the lookout for small changes they can make to improve customer satisfaction. Unfortunately, however, organizations for producing goods or services are usually very complex systems, especially if they are of any size. There are thousands upon thousands of factors that can affect customer satisfaction, some of which you can control, and some of which you cannot. You can control what goes on in your own outfit, but not what goes on outside. The perceptions of your customers are influenced by what is on offer elsewhere, the economic climate and so on. These factors you cannot control, and to make matters worse the influence of these external factors is constantly changing. So the net result is that, although you as a manager can easily recognize the need for change, it is seldom clear what you should change – or in what way.

Even when you do make a change, it is sometimes difficult so see whether it is an improvement or not, because there may be a delay before the results feed through, or because when the results do arrive they may be swamped by the effects of external influences. Dr Eli Goldratt, a consultant to General Motors and other multinationals, puts it in a nutshell. For improvement you must decide just three things: what to change, to change to what, and how to change.

In deciding what to change we need to develop a deeper understanding of what is important in our business – the critical success factors. We also need to decide in which direction to change them. In other words we need to understand cause–effect relationships. Dr William Edwards Deming, an American statistician refers to all of this as profound knowledge. He advocates the use of simple statistical methods to isolate the few important influences from amongst the many less important ones, and to help predict the effect of changes. The Japanese certainly think Deming knew what he was talking about because, back in the early 1950s, Deming was a lecturer and consultant to hundreds of top Japanese businessmen, and they still credit much of their subsequent industrial success and economic power to his methods. He has been decorated by the Emperor and honoured with the inauguration of an annual industrial quality award in his name.

To sum up then, what we mean by a scientific approach is no more than a systematic, methodical way of collecting, analysing and interpreting information, using measurements to prove we are on the right track and to monitor our progress.

Measurements and numbers

The ultimate measure of success of course is profit, but as we saw earlier, the goal of maximizing profits is not particularly helpful in suggesting how to achieve that goal. To quote Goldratt again, he suggests that the goal should be 'to make more money now and in future.' He concedes, however, this is only a marginally better guide, and it needs breaking down into more detailed supporting goals. The three he suggests for manufacturers are raising throughput, at the same time as lowering inventory and reducing operating expense. In fact Goldratt has special definitions for throughput, inventory and operating expense, but clearly they can all be measured in terms of cash, volume or time. These measures can be charted, and thus when you make a change to the manufacturing system you can quickly see whether the change has resulted in an improvement. This is exactly the approach adopted in Japanese factories, where huge charts for monitoring key performance indicators are to be seen everywhere. By this means they are able to secure the continuous improvement of their processes, quickly cancelling any trials which cause the indicators to deteriorate, and thus consolidating and protecting all previous improvement. This is in stark contrast to the crisis management, or fire-fighting styles of management adopted in less methodical organizations, where financial problems or customer complaints result in knee-jerk responses from management who feel they must be seen to be taking decisive action. These ill-considered, short-term management reactions are likely to do as much harm as good in the long run, and in such organizations there can be no steady but continuous improvement in performance.

Collecting and presenting performance figures can be tiresome and repetitive, but computers are ideal for automating much of the task, as we shall see in Chapter 3.

Management information systems

In this introductory chapter we have taken a tour through many areas where information is used in organizations. Computers are commonplace at work now, but still only a small proportion of a manager's total information needs are supplied by computers. However, you must know from your own experience that personal computers are so cheap that department managers can buy them out of petty cash almost, and as a result they pop up like mushrooms wherever there is a need to store or process information. You know the syndrome: your records are getting in a mess and you are on the point of buying some new filing cabinets but can't find floor space for them. A couple of your more reliable staff have been going on for some time about how the records should be held on computer and so you decide to give them their chance. For you to automate on an *ad hoc* departmental basis like this is fine up to a point, because it is an efficient way of solving local problems. However, separate managers solving their individual problems like this create 'islands of information', which do nothing for the flow of information and co-operation between departments. More often than not managers end up with many different and incompatible brands of hardware and software which cannot be linked up easily, thus destroying any chance of developing a corporate information strategy. Information in the form of a printout from one computer system must then be passed to the next department where it is immediately re-keyed into their different computer system. This is an utter nonsense from a corporate point of view. It is labour intensive, time consuming and inaccurate, allowing the inevitable transcription errors to occur, but more seriously the stacks of printouts create bottlenecks in the information flow, making it impossible for the organization to respond quickly to market and customer needs.

What should happen in theory (as we shall see in Chapter 5) is that someone should take a look at the information requirements of the organization as a whole and then develop an efficient system to meet those requirements. If this is to happen it is often necessary to hire computer consultants who have experience of developing such systems. This so-called top-down planning is not entirely incompatible with the bottom-up implementation that is so common. However, if implementation is allowed to proceed too far before a plan is in place, the existing heavy investment in incompatible subsystems will pre-empt its execution.

The challenge

Technology and politics are changing the business world. You as a manager need to be aware of these changes. You need to be aware of what is going on and equip yourself with the new skills required by organizations for survival in a rapidly changing environment.

Flexibility and responsiveness are paramount, and these abilities of course depend on information – the way it is collected, processed and acted upon. In the following chapters we will examine in more detail some of the ways in which information can be managed within organizations to improve flexibility and responsiveness. Some of the topics you may find more immediately relevant than others, but study them all: they will add to your competence now as a manager and to your employability in the future, when you may wish to find work with a different organization.

Competence self-assessment

Here are some questions that may help you to focus in on any weak spots in your portfolio of managerial skills and knowledge.

1   What would you say are the main corporate objectives of your organization? Some, but not all organizations publicize a corporate mission statement which will outline these. Do you know what they are? If so, write them down.

2   List the main types of information that your organization must collect in order to meet its objectives and carry out its functions.

3   Are there any types of information that your organization should be collecting but does not? List three types of information that your organization could collect which may allow it to become more responsive to its 'customers'.

4   Do you suffer from information overload? – or shortage of information? If so, briefly describe in general terms without reference to technology, the nature of your problem.

5   Write five lines under each of the following headings to describe how your problems in question 4 could be overcome:

- Organizational structure.
- Organizational culture.
- Computers.
- Communications.
- Other considerations.

6   Write down the main changes that have taken place over the last five years to the services or products supplied by your organization. What trends do these indicate, and where could these trends lead to in another five years?

7   Write down three initiatives you should personally take, to prepare yourself for the changes you think likely in the next five years.

8   Write down three initiatives you think your organization should take, to prepare itself for the changes you think likely in the next five years.

9   Write five lines under each of the following headings to describe how each could benefit through better information management:

- Teamwork
- Quality
- Efficiency
- Effectiveness
- Speed of response

10   The total system for collecting and distributing information throughout your organization may or may not make use of computers and digital information. Suggest one local improvement, not necessarily involving computers, which you can cost-justify.

References and further reading

Buyers guide – new car prices and specifications. *What Car?*, August 1996. Haymarket Motoring Publications.

Deming, W. E. (1988). *Out of the Crisis*. Cambridge University Press.

Department of Trade and Industry. *The Route Ahead*. This is a free directory of publications and videos available from the Department of Trade and Industry. Telephone: 0171 510 0144.

Goldratt, E. M. and Cox, J. (1986). *The Goal: A Process of Ongoing Improvement*. North River Press.

Peters, T. (1992). *Liberation Management. Necessary Disorganization for the Nanosecond Nineties*. Macmillan.

Schonberger, R. J. (1990). *Building a Chain of Customers*. Hutchinson.

2 How organizations handle information

Why is this chapter relevant?

It is important for you as a manager to appreciate the information needs of your colleagues as well as your own. This chapter deals with concepts and principles, and also gives practical examples of operational information and some common ways of handling it.

The way in which organizations handle information is important because it affects just about everything they do. For instance, bureaucratic organizations are formal, slow and ponderous in the way they handle information, whereas new, small organizations with everyone working in the same room perhaps, tend to be less formal, fast and flexible.

Specialists who study the way organizations handle information used to be called O&M analysts and they spent most of their time designing pro-forma forms, reports and other paperwork. Their modern equivalents are known as systems analysts and designers. They also spend most of their time thinking about how best to handle information, but that now often means getting rid of paperwork. We will take a closer look at systems in Chapter 5.

Information types and channels

Is information a corporate resource, in some ways similar to other resources such as capital equipment, raw materials, or finance? The courts seem to think so for certain types of information, such as product designs, best-sellers and computer programs, which they refer to as 'intellectual property'. This kind of information has required effort and expense to produce, and it has value because copies of it can be sold. The courts recognize the rights of ownership of this kind of property and are prepared to protect it.

But information is different from finance or capital equipment, because a particular machine can only manifest itself once, and copies are almost as difficult to make as the original, whereas a software program or a novel can be reproduced easily, millions of times if necessary. In fact the marginal cost of providing one extra copy of an information product to a customer across the Internet is actually close to zero.

We can categorize information according to its market value. Broadly, there are three types of information:

DIABETIC AUDIT – Dr M Edison & Partners @ 01/08/96

Period	Feet	Pulses	Sensation	Cholesterol	Creatinine
Dec 91	69	67	61	6	0
Jun 92	92	88	61	32	3
Dec 92	83	90	91	35	9
Jun 93	10	93	66	67	80
Dec 93	44	70	69	54	70
Jun 94	100	95	81	63	82
Dec 94	100	89	89	83	95
Jun 95	100	99	90	68	98
Dec 95	99	99	90	89	100
Jun 96	97	95	87	95	93

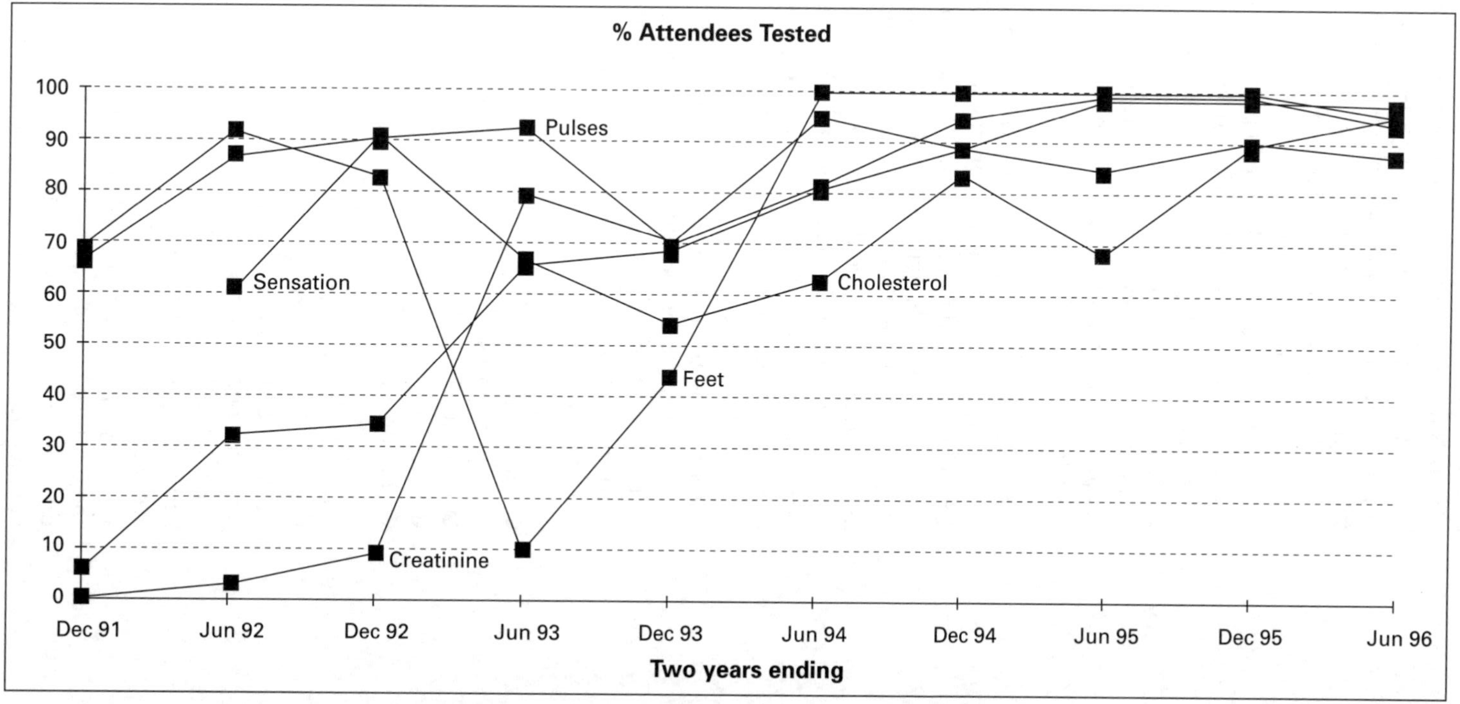

Figure 2.1 Internal information used in managing a health centre

- Information for sale, such as software which can be used, or news which informs, or a video or novel which entertains. This is usually privately owned, and access to it is sold by the owner at the market price. Often it has a limited shelf-life, its value declining with time.
- Information given freely, such as train and passenger jet timetables which has been made available by the owners, because it is in their interests to do so. Advertisements and promotional material fall into this category. Although the information itself is freely available, third parties such as publishers and database operators can often charge for access to such information.
- Information for internal use by organizations, which is never intended to be sold, and is only of legitimate value to the user, such as production schedules, sales forecasts, budgets and minutes of meetings.

All organizations use these types of information. Organizations cannot function for long without it. It is their life blood, essential for decision-making and control. It allows them to anticipate changes in an increasingly changeable business environment and to respond effectively to their clients and customers. Information on actual performance must be compared with planned performance and, in the event of a difference, appropriate action must be decided upon. Also, to maintain efficiency, information on outputs must be compared with information on inputs, so that appropriate action can be taken to improve the ratio.

As you might realize, it is the information for internal use which we are most concerned with in this book, and the value of such information is always difficult to establish, because there is no external market for it. We do know that its value depends upon factors such the following:

- relevance
- completeness
- accuracy
- clarity
- timeliness

– because these factors affect its usefulness in decision-making, and have a direct bearing on the organization's ability to respond to market needs. Today the consumer is king. That is truer now than it has ever been before.

For a time, just after the Second World War, the British public gratefully accepted whatever our own home-grown private and public sectors provided. At that time there were few imported goods and virtually no competition as manufacturers concentrated on volume at the expense of quality and prompt delivery, in their attempts to keep up with demand. And the public sector, largely protected from competition by state-granted monopolies, grew bureaucratic and unresponsive to an uncomplaining market. The poor consumer had only one choice – take it or leave it – and that applied both to goods and services.

But now tax payers expect a better deal; the public and service sectors are monitored by watchdogs such as Oftel, audited by bodies such as the Audit Commission, and exposed to competition from the private sector through privatization and compulsory competitive tendering.

New ICL computer system for post offices

The girocheques and order books used for benefits payments at 20,000 post offices in the UK, will soon be replaced by a card-based system. The project, which is being managed by Pathway, the ICL subsidiary, should be fully installed by the end of 1998.

Currently, some 890 million order book and girocheque payments are made through post offices each year. The new system should speed up counter service, and is expected to result in fraud savings of £150 million a year.

Pathway have experience with post office counter payment systems in London and the Republic of Ireland. Also they are subcontracting work for software to Oracle Corporation, for the software platform to Microsoft, and for communications to British Telecom.

John Bennett, Pathway's managing director commented: 'This is an acknowledgement of the formidable range of proven skills and expertise that the Pathway consortium offers.' He added that they looked forward to providing the basis for 'new services which will take the Post Office Counters into the next millennium.'

The net result is that all organizations are being forced to be more responsive to the needs of the consumer, who is being offered a bewildering range of alternatives by competing organizations, and will walk away – withdrawing financial support – from organizations that fail to meet their needs.

All organizations have routines for collecting and disseminating information. They may consist of simple pro-formas or logs filled out by hand at the end of each day, they may be highly automated data collection systems using the latest technology or, most often, they are something in between these extremes, combining manual and computerized, formal and informal routines.

Information can be communicated in many ways. Here are a few examples:

- Telephone – for quick, informal one-to-one communications.
- Meetings – for more formal discussions.
- Written material – for less immediate, more permanent messages, e.g. memos, reports, house journals.
- Computer networks – for e-mail
- Computer disks – for transferring data, also for training material.
- Videos – for training.
- Audio tapes – for training, also for note taking.

Information to aid decision-making

Managers make their decisions in support of the objectives of their organization. But the types of decision taken – and the information needs – are different at different levels in the organization. According to R. N. Anthony of Harvard:

- Senior managers must carry out the strategic planning. They must develop overall goals and methods of achieving them.
- Middle managers have the job of management control. They must ensure these overall goals are achieved effectively and efficiently.
- Junior managers are responsible for task or operational control. They must ensure specific tasks are carried out effectively and efficiently.

The overall picture is that, while top managers do more planning, middle and lower managers spend more time controlling those plans.

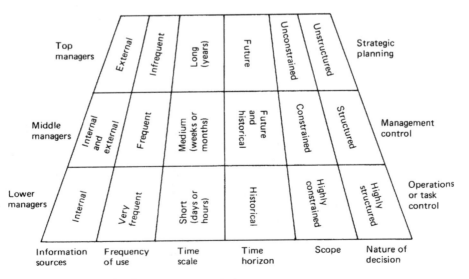

Figure 2.2 *Top managers plan; lower managers control*

Of course all managers do some planning and some controlling: it is the proportions that vary at different levels in the organization. The whole picture is summarized in Figure 2.2.

This may seem too theoretical, so let's take an example of a large manufacturing organization which has headquarters staff, and several

	Top managers (Strategic planning)	Middle managers (Management control)	Lower managers (Operations/Task control)
Job title	Operations director	Factory manager	Production manager
Typical decision	Planning new factories and new products	To find the best way to make new products. To budget for existing products	To work to sales targets. To achieve production targets
Information sources	External: sites, markets, economic and social trends	External: raw materials, new machines and labour. Internal: stocks and production	Internal: orders outstanding, resource availability and deployment
Frequency of decision	Infrequent and irregular	Every quarter, or every month perhaps for budgets	By the hour, or daily
Time scale	New factories, new products take a year or more to come on stream	Budgets are quarterly. New production lines take months to install	Production supervised hourly, monitored daily
Time horizon	Forward looking to steer the organization	Future planning and historical monitoring	Mostly historical, comparing achieved output against targets
Scope	Unconstrained. Searching for the right questions as well as the right answers. What else could or should be planned instead of new factory?	Constrained to meet the plans of top managers	Highly constrained, to meet budgets, targets, forecasts
Nature of decision	Unstructured. Often no clear precedents to follow in decision making	Semi-structured. Many decisions and plans have precedents and methodology, e.g. network analysis, budgeting	Highly structured. Well developed routines and procedures for production and operations management

Figure 2.3   *The decisions managers make*

factories. If we were to look at three managers at senior, middle and junior levels and the decisions they have to take, we might find the pattern to be like that shown in Figure 2.3.

I think it is worth pointing out, however, that R. N. Anthony's analysis described above, assumes a fairly bureaucratic organizational model, based mainly upon larger American organizations in the 1960s and 1970s. There is now a new breed of management writers who are saying that the old bureaucracies are no longer competitive in world markets. Tom Peters and others believe the new business environment of faster change and greater competition requires 'flatter' organization structures with only a skeleton headquarters staff, much less centralized control, and empowerment of people throughout the organization to change things for the better.

This new style of management will of course require information to be handled more freely and openly. It will affect the design of systems for handling information.

New organization at John Laing requires new IT

John Laing is one of Britain's largest construction companies, with a turnover of £1.3 billion. Facing intense competition, Laing developed a five-year corporate vision to decentralize the structure of the company, thus allowing core businesses to build on their strengths. This required a move away from their Comperex 895 mainframe, to free up core construction projects from dependence on centralized information resources.

'One way of staying ahead of the competition is by adapting your organization to manage the wide spectrum of customer needs. If you don't do this, your organization will suffer.' said David Jones, Group IT Director for Laing plc. 'Reorganizing your company to reflect the core business objectives is not as dramatic as it sounds. A radical change is always easier to implement as long as you tell everyone what you're doing. We went for NetWare 4 because it was a proven networking solution, and complemented the structural reorganization Laing was keen to make.' . . . 'NetWare 4 removed the need for departments to be totally dependent on accessing all information from the mainframe and saw the birth of fully autonomous units managing workloads from a localized IT set-up.'

Jones sees the benefits to the organization: 'We can provide a fully comprehensive service to our customers and we will be able to involve them far more intimately in the design and construction plans. We will use IT to improve our commercial activities not to direct them.' He adds: 'Netware 4 has reduced our costs and allowed us to maximize our in-house expertise. This has improved the way we run our projects and the quality of our final products.'

Information for competitive edge

Quality, flexibility and responsiveness are the strategic issues of today. Organizations that don't understand this new discipline are declining and will eventually disappear, as other more flexible organizations take over their role by offering better perceived value. It has already happened to much of the UK manufacturing industry as a result of increased competition from Japan and other countries during the 1970s and 1980s. Japan in particular understands the vital importance of quality and flexibility, and they are now moving into our service sectors too. For instance, in the London financial markets, Japanese banks already own more banking assets in the City than do the UK banks.

To succeed in the new era of global competition, organizations need relevant, timely and accurate information on:

- Market research, to be responsive.
- Quality control, to produce high quality.
- Progress, to deliver on time.
- Budgets and costs, to offer good value.
- Design, to offer variety.
- Sales, to match demand.

An information system is needed to co-ordinate and control the flow of information in an organization, like the nervous system of an animal. Paperwork systems used to be satisfactory, but like the dinosaurs are becoming extinct because they are too cumbersome to survive in today's world markets. For organizations of any size, a computer network is now virtually essential.

Also, the shape of the information system must reflect the chains of command and channels of communication shown on the organization chart. As we will see in Chapter 5, the architecture of the information system must be suited to the organizational structure. An information system which is designed for R. N. Anthony's type of organization is unlikely to serve well the needs of the flatter, more flexible organizations necessary for survival in today's world markets.

Information for teamwork

Tom Peters attacks the classical organization structure for encouraging people to protect their 'turf' – by which he means their function or department. The old-style organization encourages company politics, internal competition between departments and buck-passing. Organizations that behave like this are wasting energy: if they pull themselves apart like this with internal conflicts and tensions, they are unlikely to perform well in competition with other organizations where the members are pulling together as a team.

Peters is not the only one trying to get departments within organizations to work together in a spirit of co-operation rather than conflict. Richard Schonberger suggests that companies should build a 'chain of customers' right through the organization, where each person or department regards any other person or department receiving their work output, as a customer whether inside or outside the organization. The concept of the internal customer has been widely accepted as a useful concept to get departments to break down internal barriers and co-operate fully, rather than try to duck responsibility for any shortcomings, and pass the buck whenever possible.

Teams cannot function without free and open communications between their members. Without communication there can be no team, only individuals, each doing their own thing. Therefore, it is worth considering for a moment what is needed to ensure good communications between team members. There are only two essentials:

● channels, or means of communicating, and
● motivation, or desire to communicate.

– and though one can compensate for the other to some extent, both must be adequate. If, for instance, you know from experience that a colleague is difficult to get hold of on the phone, but you have a strong desire to speak to him or her, you will persist. If however, the personal cost in terms of trying unsuccessfully to get through becomes too high, you will probably give up and the communication will fail. There will be longer term effects too: in future you may not even attempt to communicate because you expect it to be too much effort, and teamwork then becomes seriously weakened.

Now suppose the channels are adequate; you know that with portable phones, voice-mail and e-mail, one way or another you will get through. But let's suppose that in the past you have found communicating with your colleague to be unsatisfactory for one reason or another, then even though the channels are adequate you probably won't communicate. You have to believe that your colleague will respect your views, value your comments and co-operate. If you know from experience that the most likely response will be stonewalling

('We can't do anything about that'), buck-passing ('You'll have to speak to Fred') or just plain rejection ('That's your problem, not ours'), then are you going to bother communicating?

So the free flow of information within an organization doesn't just depend on the channels, the systems and the technology; it also depends on the culture, the willingness to work as a team, and the level of respect we hold for our colleagues.

Teamwork, you will remember from Chapter 1, is one of the cornerstones of total quality management (TQM). Quality, as we have seen, is critically important to success, and yet some organizations still partly remove the responsibility for quality from those who produce the goods or services. They do this by setting up a quality control department which carries the can if a customer complains about quality. In fact, anyone who has any contact with the product or service can have an effect on quality. If different departments work to optimize their own separate objectives, this can lead to a result which is far from satisfactory for the organization as a whole.

The Japanese avoid this pitfall. Their organizations seem to work well as teams, using quality circles (quality improvement teams) for instance to tap into the creativity and ingenuity of their workers. We will return to the subject of quality circles and their information needs in the next chapter when we examine kaizen tools, but for now let us observe that in the same way that a power shovel amplifies physical strength, so an information system to support teamwork should amplify the intellectual capacity of the team.

Software for group communications

The Lotus Development Corporation offers software designed to improve communications within groups, or teams, of workers. They call it Lotus Notes. Here's what they say about it:

Innovative software for group communications that revolutionizes the way people work

Lotus Notes is a first – software designed for the rapid development of work group applications within a networked environment. As networks connect PCs and workstations, Notes connects work groups. With Notes, people in work groups can share critical information – within a building, nationally, and internationally in different time zones.

What's in it for you?

Lotus Notes is for people who need to share information, whether it be textual information, spreadsheets, graphics or images.

Notes provides an environment where people can work together, no matter what physical barriers separate them. Through customized applications, Notes allows people to exchange information and ideas without having to physically meet.

1 A Notes sales tracking application allows your sales team to stay active in the field, but still communicate and share vital up-to-date information with headquarters.
2 A Notes information news wire application keeps everyone informed of the latest business developments wherever they are in the world.
3 A Notes discussion database allows everyone to share information and exchange ideas without any physical meetings.

Notes adds value to an organization by harvesting the richest source of information it has – the knowledge of people within that organization. It increases the productivity of an organization because everyone is better informed and up-to-date with the latest developments.

Improved communications

Notes provides a single unifying platform that allows you seamlessly to join all of the basic types of business communication:

● One to one: electronic mail.
● One to many: distribution lists, news letters, reference libraries, news wires.
● Many to one: executive information systems, tracking systems.
● Many to many: discussion, group conferences.

Lotus Notes software (see box) is designed for teamwork, and the new, less hierarchical organizations of the information age. It is a 'groupware' product which supports co-operation, rather than the individualism which Western organizations tended to favour in the past. It opens up the free flow of information needed by multi-skilled self-managing teams, and it can help organizations make the transition from bureaucracy to less centralized control and greater flexibility of response.

Information for control

Teamwork and less centralized control may be desirable, but let us turn now to look at how many present-day organizations actually control their output.

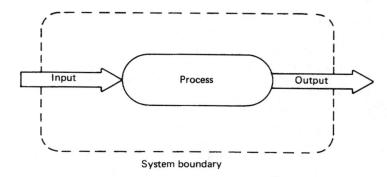

Figure 2.4   *Block diagram for a simple system*

Control system concepts

We need to define a few terms first. In control theory, we assume a 'system', which has a 'boundary'. 'Inputs' flow into a 'process' which changes them in some way and converts them into 'outputs' which flow out of the system.

A control system has another element, and that is something called 'feedback', where the output of the system is compared with some desired standard and, if there is a difference, the input or the process is adjusted in some way to bring the output back into line.

We will touch upon systems again in Chapters 4 and 5; the concept of a system is important in this subject, so let's use a familiar example.

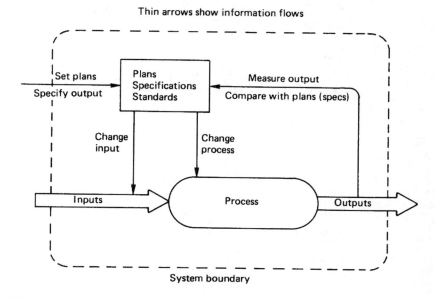

Figure 2.5   *Block diagram for a control system*

Do you have a shower at home? If so, you may just have a hot and cold tap that you have to adjust to get the right temperature, or you may have a thermostatically controlled unit. A simple tap-controlled shower is a system for producing a mixture of hot and cold water at the temperature you require, but it is not an automatic control system. You have to do the controlling, so that when someone turns on a tap somewhere else in the house, which affects the balance of inputs to your system, you have to adjust the shower taps to bring the temperature back within acceptable limits.

A thermostatically controlled shower is an automatic control system. Before you step under the shower you provide an information input by means of setting the control knob to the value, or standard required. Then, the hot and cold supplies can vary but, providing they remain within the design limits, the shower unit will automatically compensate for changes in the inputs, to provide a reasonably constant output temperature. If the temperature of the hot water input falls, the temperature of the output will begin to fall. But as soon as it does, the unit detects that there is a difference between actual output and planned output, increases the proportion of hot water in the input to compensate, and brings the output back in line with the standard.

To summarize, a simple control system has the following elements:

● Input.
● A process for modifying the input in some way.
● Output.
● A standard to which the output should conform.
● Measurement of the output.
● Comparison of the output with the standard.
● Feedback.

Strictly speaking, we should refer to this as negative feedback, because the adjustment to be made to the process or the inputs is always in the opposite direction to the error, and in proportion to the

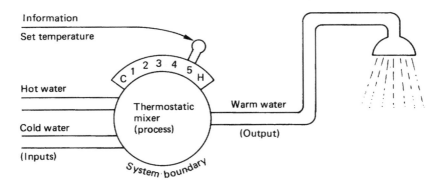

Figure 2.6 *Control system for a shower*

size of the error. For instance, if the shower water is too hot the input mixture is made cooler, and if it is very much too hot the input is made very much cooler.

Management control systems work in just the same way in principle. In production control for instance, if we have to produce 40,000 units in one month, and by the end of the first week we have produced 8000, we know that we are 2000 behind schedule because the plan requires 10,000 per week for four weeks. Negative feedback suggests that we should turn up the wick a bit – i.e. increase production because of the shortfall of actual production compared to the plan – by working overtime, or whatever means. Without early monitoring in this way, the error may get even worse and perhaps become irretrievable within the time remaining until the due date.

The routine collection of production information and comparing it against the plan is something to which computers are ideally suited, and was one of the first business applications of computers outside of the accounting and payroll functions, over twenty years ago.

Production control: materials requirement planning

Controlling the production of cars, or washing machines, or microwave ovens, involves more than just counting the number of finished items each week and then working some overtime if the number is less than planned. To put together a complex assembly of parts regularly and in large quantities involves detailed logistics to ensure that the right quantities of components are available when required, and that the right amounts of raw materials are available to make those components.

The software used to handle these problems is called MRP (materials requirement planning) software, and has three main inputs:

● The MPS, or master production schedule.
● The BOM, or bill of materials.
● The current inventory, or level of stocks and their delivery lead-times, from the inventory file.

Remember, the purpose of MRP software is to achieve the MPS (the planned future output per week), but at the same time to control levels of raw materials and work-in-progress (WIP) so that stock-outs do not occur.

The printouts consist of:

● Reports to production, telling what should be produced and when.
● Reports to purchasing, telling what to buy and when.

It works like this. The MPS is determined by sales and marketing, partly from forecasted sales, and partly from orders received. It

On-hand inventory at end of August = 100

Month	September				October				Nov	
Week No.	37	38	39	40	41	42	43	44	45	46
Forecast demand (gross requirements)	150	150	160	160	150	140	140	140	120	
Projected on-hand inventory (gross availability)	200	50	140	230	80	190	50	160	40	
Production planned (receipts) MPS	250		250	250		250		250		

To find projected on-hand inventory, add on-hand inventory for the preceding week to production planned for the current week. Then subtract forecast demand.

Figure 2.7   *Master production schedule for a table lamp*

consists of a schedule of numbers of finished assemblies to be produced each week:

The BOM for a product is a kind of structured parts list, in the form of a hierarchy, with the top level (level 0), being the finished assembly. The next level down (level 1), consists of the major sub-assemblies from which the final assembly is put together. Level 2 shows the parts from which the subassemblies are made, and level 3 may be materials from which the parts are made. For instance, a table lamp might have a BOM like the one shown in Figure 2.8.

You will probably realize that the BOM contains information on how the product is actually made. There are sometimes choices as to how the product is assembled, and this will affect the BOM. For instance, should the plug be put on the flex before the flex is put on the lamp, or afterwards? Also, the greater the complexity of the final assembly, and the more operations there are to be performed, the greater the number of levels in the BOM. For instance, if our table lamp manufacturer just puts together parts and subassemblies made by outside contractors, the BOM may only have three or four levels. If, however, the company makes the parts in several stages from raw materials, builds them into sub-subassemblies, then subassemblies and final assemblies, then the BOM may have twice as many levels.

The third input to the MRP system is the inventory file, which keeps a tally of raw materials and WIP, together with the lead-times for replenishment, either by making or buying from outside. The lead-times for manufacturing are, of course, influenced by the size of batch ordered. The software assumes a batch size which strikes a balance between the costs of holding large batches in stock, and the high costs of changing over the machines and losing productive capacity when many different small batches are planned.

Product structure diagram

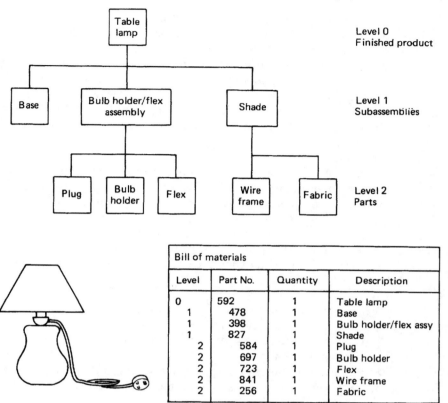

Figure 2.8 *Bill of materials (BOM) for a table lamp*

Bill of materials			
Level	Part No.	Quantity	Description
0	592	1	Table lamp
1	478	1	Base
1	398	1	Bulb holder/flex assy
1	827	1	Shade
2	584	1	Plug
2	697	1	Bulb holder
2	723	1	Flex
2	841	1	Wire frame
2	256	1	Fabric

When the MRP system is run it produces, from the master production MPS, a time-phased assembly schedule, by working backwards from the amounts required each week in the MPS. It takes into account the lead-times to find out when the subassemblies must be started if they are to be ready for final assembly. Then, working backwards in time again, the software computes when the parts must be started if they are to be ready for making into subassemblies. And, of course, the materials must be ordered soon enough for them to arrive in time to be made into parts.

By chaining back like this, the software works out when to release purchase orders to suppliers, and works orders to the shop floor for manufacture.

In fact, with just a simple product like a table lamp, a production assistant could probably keep tabs on the logistics. But in a manufacturing plant with a range of complex products, each with its own MPS, and some perhaps using the same subassemblies, the calculations rapidly become unmanageable without a computer.

Some disadvantages of MRP

MRP packages have been around for twenty years and more now. They were the only way we knew of handling the logistics of assembly for complex product ranges. However, they require very heavy investment in hardware, software, maintenance and training. Typically, it may take half a million pounds to install, and take a year for an average sized company to get up and running with MRP.

There are many different proprietary brands of MRP, but most of them work in time units (called time buckets) of one week, and assume batch production. Taken together, these two factors mean that, even though levels of inventory and WIP are 'controlled', there must still be substantial amounts of WIP about for the system to function. So a company that installs MRP may be committing itself for the life of the system to working with substantial amounts of WIP. It may be possible to work with smaller rather than larger batch sizes, but even so this is not ideal at a time when firms are working towards systems of just-in-time (JIT) production using batch sizes of one unit.

Working with a high level of WIP has several serious disadvantages:

● It ties up capital.
● It makes design changes difficult.
● It makes it difficult to adjust the throughput rate to match sudden changes in demand.
● It allows poor quality manufacture, whereas JIT will not. With JIT, the whole factory stops when a faulty part is produced – a strong incentive to produce zero defects.

Project control: critical path method

In manufacturing, controlling the flow of products is all-important. In the service sector it is teams and activities that must be co-ordinated and controlled. In both, however, there are due-dates to be met. In manufacturing, MRP is used to work back from the due-date to find out when to start work on products, and in the service sector a similar technique can be used to determine when activities should be scheduled to start and finish. The technique is called network analysis or critical path analysis. If you work in the service sector, I hope you will not be too dismayed to learn that this technique originated in the manufacturing sector, but it has been found to be perhaps even more useful in the service sector. Have you ever started a project with lots of different things to be done before the due-date deadline? If so, you will surely understand the basic principles upon which critical path analysis is based – which are, scheduling forward from the present, and scheduling back from the due-date, to see if everything can be fitted into the time available.

Critical path analysis dates back to the 1950s when after the Second World War several very large projects were under way in the USA, and these were presenting new problems of co-ordination and planning. It is in the nature of projects that they last only for a period of time, during which many different teams and types of activity have to be co-ordinated and brought to a successful conclusion by the due-date. Two groups of researchers were addressing these problems and they came up with variants of essentially the same technique, the best known of which is PERT, which stands for program evaluation and review technique. PERT was used to control the US Navy's Polaris Missile development programme and was credited with bringing forward the completion date by two whole years.

Few managers get involved with projects as big as Polaris, but PERT can be just as effective in controlling smaller projects such as launching a new service or product, installing a computer system and training staff to use it, or launching a sales training programme.

Here's a simple example to illustrate how it works. Suppose you are in charge of a team responsible for arranging a sales training programme for your organization. You have listed all the components of the project. These are the things or 'activities' that members of your team must do, and the times needed for doing them – the activity 'durations' in days:

List locations	2
Select locations	4
Plan topics	3
Get speakers	7
Arrange speaker travel plans	5
Design and print brochure	14
Final check on travel plans	8
Take reservations	6
Run training programme	10

The technique has three phases:

- The planning phase, when you decided what activities will make up the project.
- The analysis phase, when you use the computer to schedule the activities.
- The control phase, when you monitor the project and hold it to plan.

Planning

In our example, the planning phase is complete, and the results are shown in the table above.

Analysis

During the analysis phase, we must show if some activities are dependent on other activities being completed first. For instance in building a house, you cannot plaster the walls until the walls are built, so plastering must be scheduled to follow on in series after wall-building. However, there will be other independent activities as well. For instance, once the walls have been built the plumber and electrician need not work in any special order. Either can work before the other, or they can work side by side in parallel. Returning now to our sales training programme, clearly the speaker travel plans cannot be arranged until the locations have been finalized. This is a dependent relationship. However, it is OK for the speaker travel plans to be arranged at the same time as the brochure is being prepared, because these activities are independent.

Project managers used to sort out all these logical relationships by using arrows to represent activities, with the dependent arrows chaining across the page one after the other, and the independent activities shown in parallel. This created a kind of network effect, with the arrows fanning out from the start point on the left of the page, and then converging onto the finish point on the right-hand side. Just a few years ago the network used to be the main analytical device for determining the critical path – the longest chain of activities through the network, which of course is the shortest time in which the whole project can be completed. It was the main device for scheduling all the activities, but the network was a poor device for communicating the schedule to those who were responsible for performing the activities, and so the results were usually displayed in the form of a Gantt chart (horizontal bar chart).

Until recently, you needed to combine expert draughting skills with a degree in logic if you wanted to draw up a network, as you can see from the old example of a chemical plant construction project, shown in Figure 2.9.

Now, however, computers do it all, rescuing thousands of business students and project managers from ever again having to draw up a network chart. All that's necessary is for you to enter the list of component activities along with their durations, and then link together any dependent activities in the appropriate order. Then at the click of a mouse, you can display or print out the schedule either as a PERT network or as a Gantt chart (see Figures 2.10 and 2.11). And what is more, you can enter the human resources assigned to each activity on dozens of different projects, and the computer will avoid clashes where the same resource might be at risk of being called for by several activities at the same time. So the computer has converted what used to be a somewhat limited and laborious technique into a simple, powerful tool for supporting many aspects of a project manager's routine.

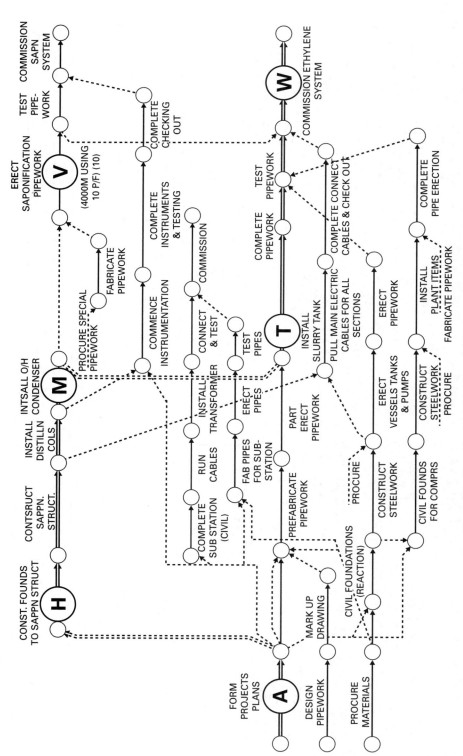

Figure 2.9 Network of activities for a plant construction project

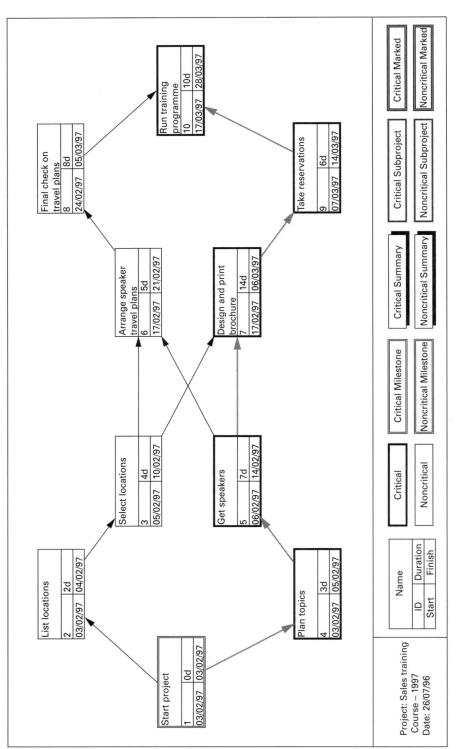

Figure 2.10 *Network for arranging a sales training programme (prepared using Microsoft Project software)*

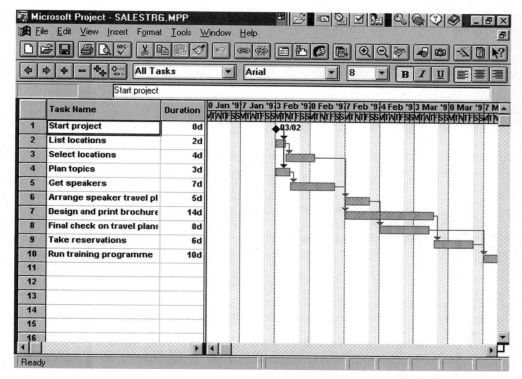

Figure 2.11 *The screen display produced by Microsoft's project planning software. The project manager's view of the training programme project*

Control

If a critical activity (one lying on the critical path) is delayed by so much as a day, the whole project will be delayed by the same amount. Non-critical activities, however, lie on shorter chains through the network and have more time available than is strictly necessary for their completion, so it probably won't matter if they overrun by a day or two. Typically, perhaps less than a quarter of all the activities in a project may turn out to be critical, and that is what makes this technique so popular with managers. It allows you to focus your limited time and attention on those few activities where it will be most effective. During this control phase it is important to make sure everyone knows when they are working on critical activities, and the importance of sticking to schedule.

Some names of commonly used software are: Microsoft Project, Plantrac II from Computerline Ltd, SuperProject Expert from Computer Associates, and Artemis from Metier. There are many other excellent packages available, too numerous to mention them all.

Competence self-assessment

Here are some questions to help you consolidate what you have learned from this chapter, and relate it to your own experience at work.

1   Under the headings of 'Regular' and 'Occasional', list the channels and types of communication you receive while doing your job. For instance, a regular channel through which you will probably receive information is the phone, and possibly the type of information might be sales enquiries.

2   List the main activities that occupied you at work last week, or that occupy you during a typical week. Estimate the percentage of your time during that week which you spent on each of the following activities: strategic planning, management control and operational control. From this analysis, would R. N. Anthony classify you as a junior, a middle or a senior manager?

3   Give an example of a decision you often have to make at work with inadequate information. What extra information would make the decision easier or safer? What can you do to arrange for more information to be available next time?

4   Who inside your organization receives work that you do? Do you regard them as your customers? If you were to ask them how you could improve the quality of service or product that you deliver to them, how would they answer?

5   Are you required to operate to an annual budget? Do you have regular monthly or quarterly budget reviews? If so, use systems terminology to describe these features as parts of a financial control system.

6   The table below lists in the first column the seven activities making up a complete project. In the second column are the activities that immediately precede each activity, and in the third column are the durations of each activity in weeks.

(a) By hand, draw the network for these activities. (You don't need the durations for this. Also, remember that the activity letters should be put on the activity arrows, not the event circles. Make sure all the arrows point forwards to the right.)

(b) Divide each event circle with a vertical line. Now do a forward pass through the network, starting at the first event on the left and working to the right. Put in the earliest time each event can

Table 1

Activity reference	Depends on	Duration
A	–	2
B	–	5
C	–	1
D	B	10
E	A,D	3
F	C	6
G	E,F	8

occur on the left half of each event circle. Remember that an event cannot occur until all routes through to that event have been completed. Thus the earliest event time for each event is equal to the length of the longest route through to that event.

(c) What is the shortest time that the project can be completed in? It is the same as the earliest event time for the last event on the right.

(d) Now fill in the latest event times by doing a backward pass, starting at the last event on the right and working back towards the left. Put the latest event times in the right half of each event circle. The final event on the right will have a latest event time equal to its earliest event time if the project is to be completed in the shortest possible period. The penultimate event(s) will have a latest event time equal to the latest event time of the final event less the duration of the activity in between. If there is more than one path leading back to an earlier event, it is the longest path that should be used to find its latest event time.

(f) Mark up the critical path. It is easily recognized as the sequence of activities linking all the events which have their earliest event time equal to their latest event time.

---

7 A promoter wishes to present a summer concert in the gardens of a mansion near Oxford. She decides to use PERT to help manage the project, and the time estimates for the activities are as follows:

Table 2

Activity reference	Description	Immediate predecessor	Time estimate
A	Select musicians	–	5
B	Contracts with agents	A	10
C	Arrange travel and accommodation	B	14
D	Radio, adverts, promotion	B	7
E	Print tickets, programmes	B	6
F	Sell tickets	D, E	21
G	Confirm travel and accommodation	C	11
H	Hire ticket sellers	C	16
J	Rehearsals	H	2
K	Present concert	G, F, J	3

(a) Draw the network for the project and indicate which activities lie on the critical path.

(b) What is the shortest time that the project can be completed in? How might knowing this be useful to the organizer?

(c) If the project is delayed, it may be necessary to reduce the project duration by shortening an activity. One such proposal is to contract out the ticket selling so that activity H takes only one day. What effect would this have on the expected project duration?

8 Prepare a critical path network for the following activities involved in the preparation of a cheese and pickle sandwich. Assume you have as many helpers as necessary. Determine the critical path, and calculate what the shortest 'project' time will be. Of all the activities originating from the first event in the network, which one could have the latest starting time? How late could it start?

Table 3

Activity	Duration (seconds)
Get bread from bin	60
Unwrap and cut two slices of bread	50
Get cheese from refrigerator	40
Cut one slice of cheese	50
Get pickle from cupboard	240
Put pickle in assembled sandwich	40
Get butter from refrigerator	80
Put butter on two slices of bread	70
Assemble two buttered slices and cheese	40
Cut sandwich in two and serve	40

9 A manufacturer of consumer electronics, in conjunction with an advertising agency, is planning an advertising project to launch a new personal computer. The project will involve newspaper and television advertising and will conclude with a press conference. The project activities are as follows:

Table 4

Activity	Description	Time (weeks)	Depends on
A	Plan campaign		–
B	Contracts with newspapers	3	A
C	Write text	3	A
D	Take photographs	4	C
E	Prepare artwork	2	D
F	Artwork to newspapers	1	B, E
G	Contract with film maker	3	A
H	Contracts with TV companies	3	A
J	Write film script	4	A
K	Make film	6	J, G
L	Film to TV company	1	H, K
M	Arrange press conference	2	F, L

Draw a network for the advertising project. Show which activities are critical. What is the total project duration?

The agency wishes to shorten the overall project time, and is considering the following ideas:

(a) The photographs for the newspaper advertisements can be taken while the accompanying text is being written.
(b) By allocating extra resources, the duration for agreeing the film contract can be shortened.
(c) By allocating extra resources, the duration for making the film can be shortened.

Which one of these should the agency choose in order to shorten the project? How many weeks can be saved?

References and further reading

Anthony, R. N., Dearden, J. and Bedford, N. M. (1990). *Management Control Systems* (5th edition). Irwin.

Project Management Today. Monthly magazine published by Larchdrift Projects Ltd.

Schonberger, K. (1994). *Operations Management: Continuous Improvement* (5th edition). Irwin.

3 Information and personal effectiveness

Why is this chapter relevant?

Do you want to be a better manager? There are some simple techniques described here which can help you use information to make better decisions, and communicate better with your colleagues. Decision-making and communication are functions that lie at the very heart of management. By learning these techniques, your competence as a manager will immediately benefit.

Often management information is in the form of numerical values, best understood and communicated as charts. In this chapter you can read how to draw these by hand, and also how to produce them on your personal computer (PC). However, unless you are something of an artist, you will probably end up with a better job using the computer. Also, PC-generated charts are easier to squirt down the net to your colleagues.

How to analyse and present information effectively

You, as a manager must achieve results through people. The only way you can do this is by communicating with them, that is, giving them information. If you favour – and can get away with – an autocratic management style, the information you give may be in the form of instructions. Nowadays, however, it is much more likely that you will have to persuade your staff to work the way you want by selling them ideas, rather than telling them what to do, but this need not be difficult. Very often, by presenting the facts in an obvious format, the ideas will sell themselves. Then, appropriate action is easy to see and nobody needs telling what to do. Most people will obey what Mary Parker Follet called 'the law of the situation' and just get on and do it.

Most of the techniques that will be described are very simple: anyone can understand and use them. They consist of little more than structured ways of displaying information. You can use them, and you should encourage your staff to use them. When the Japanese have demonstrated how effective they can be, it is a mystery to me why more Western organizations do not make greater use of them. Have we more of our fair share of 'flat-earthers', or do we just have inadequate levels of management training?

Kaizen tools

Know what these are? If you work for Nissan in Sunderland you would do because all employees – not just managers – are given their own Kaizen Manual explaining what they are and how to use them. The word kaizen is Japanese, but the tools themselves, with one exception, were all invented in the West, and they are essential to the process of improvement. Indeed without their widespread use it would have been impossible for Japan to rise phoenix-like from the nuclear ashes of the Second World War to her present dominant position in many world markets. The tools include:

- Pie, bar and scatter diagrams.
- Pareto diagrams.
- Ishikawa diagrams.
- The normal curve, and standard deviation.
- $\overline{X}$ and R charts.

Japanese employees at all levels organized in small groups, called quality circles, use these tools routinely to analyse and improve their work. The many small improvements being initiated everywhere result in a never-ending, relentless advance. That is what the word kaizen means – a constant gradual universal process of improvement. It is like a religion: a shared commitment to find a better future.

Of course, Kaizen tools on their own won't guarantee a one-way ticket to success in world markets, but they are essential for a proper scientific, analytical approach which, along with teamwork and an obsession with quality, form the basis of total quality management (TQM), the Western equivalent of kaizen. TQM consultants Joiner Associates of Wisconsin USA promote the idea by means of the Joiner triangle (Figure 3.1).

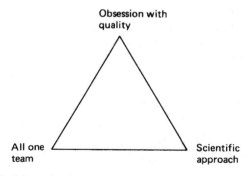

Figure 3.1 *The Joiner triangle*

Teamwork and an obsession with quality in an organization require major cultural changes which can only be started by the chief executive, but anyone can use a scientific approach to make changes based on sound evidence. And that's where the Kaizen tools come in: they're reliable methods for analysing evidence.

So is this scientific management all over again – F. W. Taylor's discredited ideas of seventy years ago? It is true that Elton Mayo's famous experiments at the Hawthorne Works of Western Electric, Illinois, showed that treating humans like machines just doesn't work, but some of Taylor's approach did survive in work study and ergonomics. The scientific method is OK; it is the way we apply it that we sometimes get wrong. After all, scientists of every discipline used it very effectively for 300 years before Taylor came along.

The scientific method was first proposed by the philosopher and former Lord Chancellor Francis Bacon during the reign of King James I. He argued that you can't deduce everything about the universe just from logic without experimenting. Later, others including Isaac Newton refined the method which basically has four steps:

● Observe an effect.
● Guess its cause.
● Test your theory by experimenting.
● Prove a relationship between cause and effect.

However, there are critics who say that even science doesn't operate strictly according to this method and, besides, for busy managers it all sounds a bit too academic. That's why 91-year-old quality guru Dr Deming proposed the PDCA, or plan–do–check–amend cycle, which the Japanese have taken to heart and used to such effect, and why IBM uses a similar four-step cycle: analyse–solve–implement–maintain, as part of their market-driven quality programme. These cycles and the one used by 'learning organizations', question–theory–test–reflection, are all loosely based on Bacon's original supposition, and they all require evidence to be analysed and small experiments or tests to be carried out, to discover how to improve. This is what the kaizen tools are for.

Pie, scatter and bar diagrams

In the UK, we use these for reports and presentations. But in TQM organizations, quality circles use them to analyse evidence and gain insight into problems (Figure 3.2).

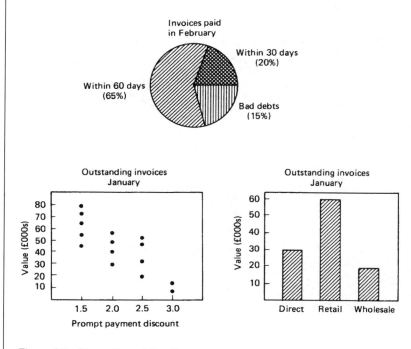

Figure 3.2 *Pie, scatter and bar diagrams*

Pareto diagrams

Vilfredo Pareto, an Italian economist, showed that it was common for about 20 per cent of nationals to own about 80 per cent of the wealth of a nation. These proportions crop up in many other circumstances too. Quality circles use the diagrams for 80/20 analysis to rank items and separate the vital few items from amongst the many other items which are also important, but less so. It is a simple but powerful technique for focusing your attention where it can be most effective.

Ishikawa diagrams

The Japanese professor Kaouru Ishikawa invented these, which are also known as cause–effect diagrams, or fishbone diagrams (Figure 3.4). They help quality circles to develop a comprehensive view of factors that might influence a problem.

Normal curve and standard deviation

These are fundamental to the study of variation. If you are serious about improving quality, you have no option but to get familiar with the normal curve and its standard deviation

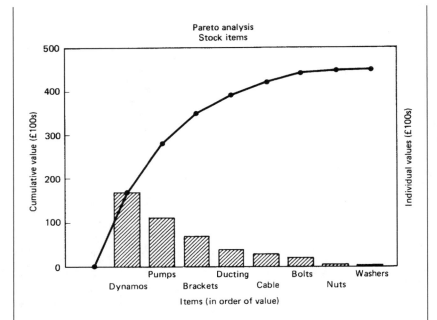

Figure 3.3   *Pareto diagram*

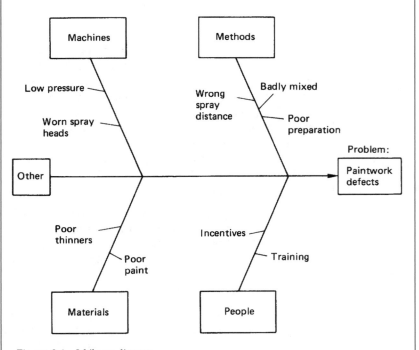

Figure 3.4   *Ishikawa diagram*

(Figure 3.5) Why? Because top quality is impossible with high variation and to reduce variation is the same as to improve quality. High variation means low predictability. If a product or service varies each time you supply it, your customers can't know what to expect, and quality assurance is all about meeting and exceeding your customers' expectations. For instance, in a supermarket, shopping can take just twenty minutes – or as much as an hour if long queues form. This is high variation and low predictability, which most customers will seek to avoid. Some will shop elsewhere to avoid the risk of an hour-long ordeal, even when shopping elsewhere takes longer on average.

Variation can be of two types: that due to a single, special, assignable cause, and that due to many common, unassignable causes which usually cancel out but occasionally stack up one way or the other. Unfortunately, in practice it is difficult to tell the two apart, and if you treat a chance stacking up of common causes believing it to be a special cause – or vice versa – you will actually increase the amount of variation and make the situation worse! For example, suppose you are in a rifle target shooting competition and you want to maximize your score with five shots. If you were to fire all five shots without adjusting the sights you wouldn't expect all the shots to go through the same hole in the target; there will be some natural variation due to common causes, and the shots will form a group of five holes – not too far apart, one hopes. Now suppose you start the competition knowing that your sights are reasonably well but

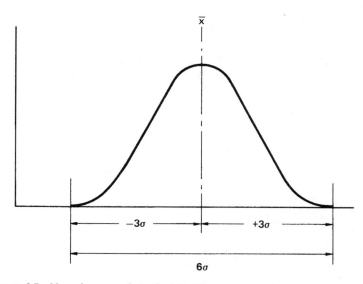

Figure 3.5 *Normal curve and standard deviation*

perhaps not perfectly adjusted, and the first shot falls a little to the left of the bull's-eye. You could adjust the sights to compensate before firing the next shot, and continue like that each time compensating for the error of the previous shot. Or, you could fire all five shots without adjusting the sights, and in fact this will result in a tighter grouping and a higher score.

Treating common causes variation as if it were a special cause is what Dr Deming refers to as tampering with the process. In business, a manager who makes an immediate adjustment to procedures because a single customer has complained is tampering. The knee-jerk reaction of the macho manager usually does more harm than good in the long run. Many UK managers don't understand these statistical concepts: all Nissan employees are encouraged to learn about them.

$\overline{X}$ and R charts

These can be used for monitoring our processes for supplying services and products. The average and range within samples of five are charted, making it possible to distinguish between common and special causes, and detect even slight changes in a process before it results in out-of-spec output. The charts are simple to use, but do require some statistical knowledge to set up. You may hear the term 'six-sigma' bandied about by employees from IBM, Motorola and other TQM companies. What they are referring to is the range of common cause variation which is controlled by using $\overline{X}$ and R-charts (Figure 3.6).

These then are some of the kaizen tools needed to support the myriad of small experiments which should be going on at all levels everywhere in your organization if it is to keep up with rising customer expectations.

Survival is not a foregone conclusion, as some big world airlines are discovering during this recession. But British Airways

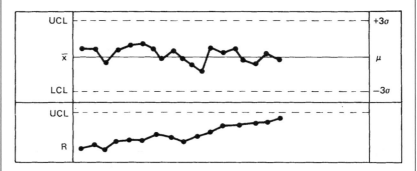

Figure 3.6 $\overline{X}$ and R charts

who were in deep trouble in 1981, losing £200 per minute through that year, became profitable in 1984 following the decision of chief executive Sir Colin Marshall to introduce TQM and, as the world's favourite airline, it is still profitable even in the current difficult conditions.

Sir Colin encourages everyone to make small experiments, recognizing that many of these will fail, but will always add to knowledge. The organizational culture must support experimentation: people must be prepared to take small risks and not be afraid of the errors that come with trial and error. That is why Sir Colin's slogan is 'Practise walking on water on shallow ponds'.

Communicating information

A technical model of communication is often portrayed as shown in Figure 3.7. This simple model has three stages:

- A sender prepares and transmits . . .
- A message via some medium to . . .
- A receiver receives and understands the message, thus completing the communication process.

Or does it? A managerial model of communication should have a fourth stage: action. The essence of management is getting results through people. It is not enough, therefore, if the receivers of your message just receive and understand it. This must behave differently in some desired way from how they would otherwise have behaved. That is the ultimate test of effectiveness.

So how can you improve your chances of securing action? Well, you must design your message to achieve two things when it is received:

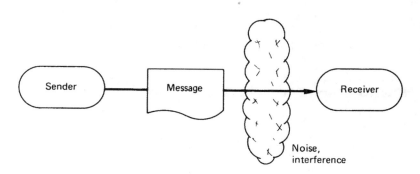

Figure 3.7   *A model of the communication process*

● It must be understood, so keep your message simple, uncluttered, and free from ambiguities or uncertainties.
● It must be interesting and relevant to your readers.

Authors on the subject generally agree that effective communication is very difficult to achieve. When figures are a significant part of the message, it adds an extra difficulty, so don't be discouraged if you find it hard.

Whenever you communicate, you are selling – you want your audience to take some kind of action in the same way as the salesperson wants the prospect to reach for his or her cheque book. Organizations function more effectively when managers view other managers in their organization as internal customers for their services. If you want to be a better manager, learn to be a better 'ideas salesperson'.

Using the kaizen tools

Like any skill, practice makes perfect, and doing something for the first time is always the most difficult. Remember when you first learned to ride a bike? But now you know you can go back and ride one anytime, even if you haven't been near a bike for years.

When you learned how to ride, you watched someone else do it first, then had a go yourself. So, in that tradition, here are some examples of how to use the kaizen tools, with lots of help and detailed guidance each step of the way. In the self-assessment section at the end of this chapter you will find exercises with less help, for you to test your understanding.

You can follow through the examples here and copy them yourself first if you wish or, if you prefer, just read through and then try the exercises. You can do them manually or by computer. The computer instructions are fairly general as the specific keystrokes necessary for achieving various effects will vary according to the particular spreadsheet available to you. Where it is necessary to give specific instructions, they will be for Microsoft Excel Version 7.0 for Windows 95.

If you are unfamiliar with PCs and spreadsheets, do the exercises manually and read Chapter 4 first, before trying to follow the computer instructions in this chapter.

How to draw a pie chart

The pie chart is ideal for breaking down a grand total into its components to show their relative sizes (Figure 3.8). For instance:

● Total sales, made up from Northern, Midlands, Southern, and Export divisions.

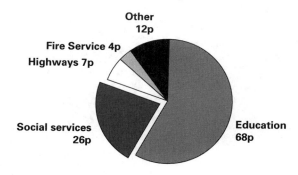

Oxfordshire County Council spending 1996–97

Other
12p

Fire Service 4p

Highways 7p

Social services
26p

Education
68p

£1.17 a day if your home is in band C

Figure 3.8   *The pie chart*

- Total council spending, on education, social services, highways etc.
- Total costs, on labour, materials, transport, overheads, etc.

You should try to restrict yourself to four or five slices at most, or the chart will become cluttered with detail and lose impact. If you must include the detail, put it in a table later on for those who are interested.

Manually

To prepare a pie chart manually is awkward, because you need some drawing instruments which may not be to hand, and the final result will depend upon your drawing skills. The minimum you need are a pencil, a ruler, a pair of compasses and a protractor. (You may have to raid your daughter's or son's pencil case for the protractor!) A calculator would be useful too. The steps are as follows:

1 Draw a circle.
2 Calculate the angle for the first slice. To do this you calculate the proportion of the total that the first component represents, and work out this proportion of 360 degrees. For instance, suppose you have the following figures:

Fixed costs	250
Variable costs	270
Overheads	230
Total	750

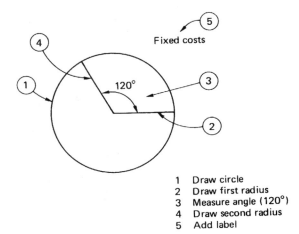

1 Draw circle
2 Draw first radius
3 Measure angle (120°)
4 Draw second radius
5 Add label

Figure 3.9 *Drawing a pie chart: stage 1*

The whole pie represents the 750, and each slice must be sized in proportion. The first slice is the fixed costs of 250. These are one-third of the total 750, and so you need to draw a slice which is one-third of the whole pie circle – in other words, one-third of 360 degrees, which is 120 degrees.

3 Now draw the slice for these fixed costs, by first drawing a radius from the centre of the circle to the right until it touches the outside of the circle. Now use your protractor to measure 120 degrees round the circle from this radius and draw a second radius. Label this slice 'Fixed costs' (Figure 3.9).

4 Next calculate the size of the second slice, as follows:

$$(270/750) \times 360 = 129.6$$

The second slice should be 129.6 degrees, but 130 degrees is perfectly close enough. Again, measure 130 degrees round the pie from your second radius and draw in the third radius. Label this slice 'Variable costs', and the remainder of the pie 'Overheads' (Figure 3.10).

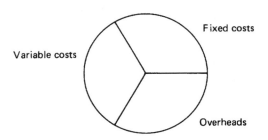

Figure 3.10 *Drawing a pie chart: stage 2*

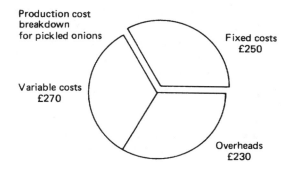

Figure 3.11   *Drawing a pie chart: stage 3*

And that's it; the pie chart is finished. You can jazz it up a bit to make it more visually interesting by adding a title and colouring it in if you wish, but don't make it too complicated. The essence of good communication is to keep things simple (Figure 3.11).

By computer

A more satisfactory way is to use a PC with spreadsheet software. With Microsoft Excel, for instance, all you need do is list on the

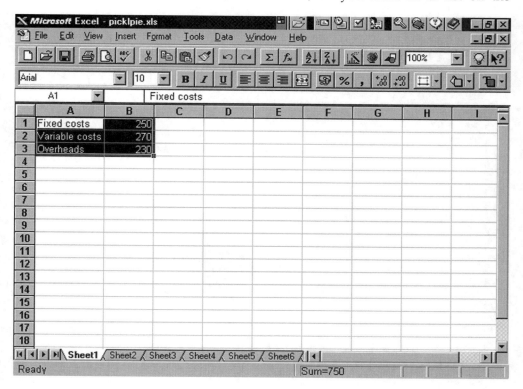

Figure 3.12   *The cost categories typed into a spreadsheet (Microsoft Excel)*

spreadsheet grid the component names and their values in two adjacent columns. Then tell the computer how you want the information displayed. The way to do this varies according to the software you are using, but if you use the Chart Wizard in Excel for instance, it's a breeze. For the same figures we used in the manual exercise, the steps are as follows:

1 Type the cost categories and values into two adjacent columns in the spreadsheet, and highlight both columns by clicking and dragging from the top left of the table down and across to the bottom right of the table (Figure 3.12).
2 Click the Chart Wizard button, and make selections in the series of dialogue boxes that follow, and presto! There's your pie-chart.
3 Now if you want to change something, just double-click on the chart to edit it, then click on the detail you want to change, and you can customize it. You can add some embellishments: a two-line title, and choose different cross-hatching, or colours for the slices. You can even pull out slightly, one or more slices of the pie, to add impact.

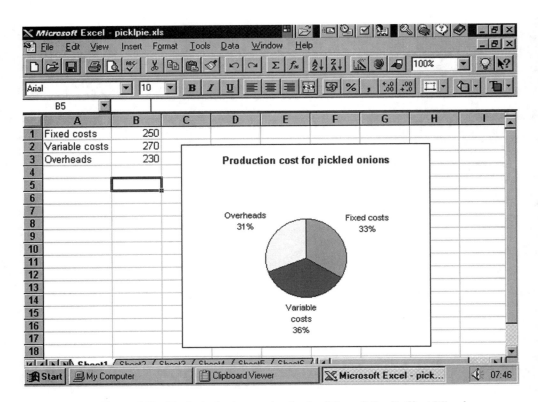

Figure 3.13 *The basic chart, as produced using Microsoft Excel's Chart Wizard*

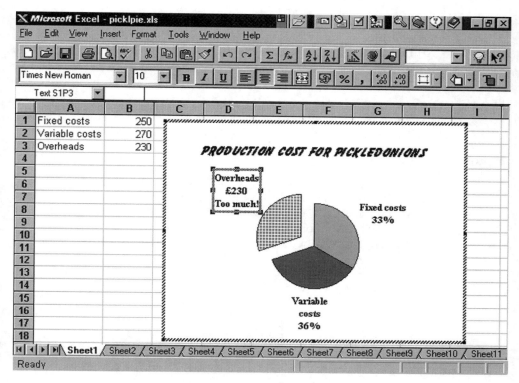

Figure 3.14   *Modifying selected elements of the basic chart*

Production cost for pickled onions

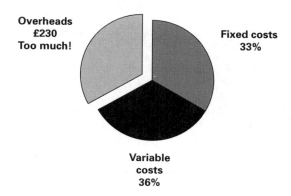

Figure 3.15   *The finished pie chart, after printing*

Without doubt, charts are the most powerful way of presenting numerical information in your reports. The best way of transferring graphs from Excel into Word (or another Windows word processor) is by copying your graph to the clipboard as a 'picture', and then pasting it in at the desired position. This will ensure it looks just as you expect it to do, and will also produce the highest print quality.

Use the Help facility to learn the specific mouse clicks and keyboard presses to invoke these commands. It is not difficult and, like riding a bicycle, once learned, your new skills tend to become almost instinctive.

How to draw a bar chart

Let's use the same figures we used for the pie chart.

Manually

A bar chart is easier to do manually than a pie chart, because you don't need to mess with compasses and protractors. You need a vertical scale up to a nice round figure larger than the largest component – 300 is suitable for our example. Then, just draw vertical bars at the appropriate height against the scale (Figure 3.16).

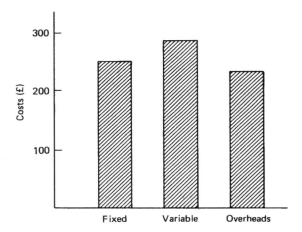

Figure 3.16   *Drawing a bar chart*

By computer

With Excel it is still much easier. The steps are the same as for the pie chart, but you make different choices in the Chart Wizard dialogue boxes (Figure 3.17). As before you can modify the basic Chart Wizard offering, before you print it out (Figure 3.18).

How to draw a scatter diagram

The scatter diagram is useful for investigating whether, or showing that there is, a relationship between two different measurements. For instance you might want to check whether monthly sales tend to increase when you increase your monthly spend on advertising. You should expect some kind of positive relationship. (Positive means that when one measurement increases, the other does too; negative means

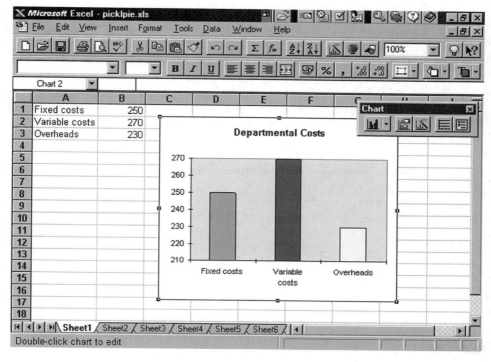

Figure 3.17   *The bar chart as produced by Excel's Chart Wizard*

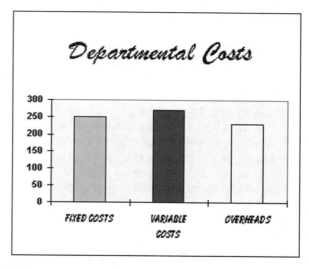

Figure 3.18   *The modified bar chart, as printed*

that one decreases as the other increases.) However, the relationship may not necessarily be perfectly clear, as other factors can influence your sales as well as the money you spend on advertising. Bad weather can have a negative effect and so can your competitors' spending on advertising, whereas a fall in interest rates may have a positive effect. These other external influences – uncontrolled variables – tend to obscure the effect of your advertising, and sometimes it is only by charting sales against advertising that we can see the trend which suggests a positive relationship.

So let's see how you would you go about preparing a scatter diagram, if your spending on advertising and the corresponding sales for the last nine months were as follows:

Table 1

Month	Advertising (£)	Sales (£000s)
Jan	5000	80
Feb	6500	42
Mar	1900	52
Apr	3000	51
May	7800	69
June	9000	90
July	3500	55
Aug	6000	60
Sept	7900	120

Manually

When preparing a scatter diagram you should always put the controlled variable – advertising in this case – along the bottom, or x-axis. The dependent variable, sales, will then rise or fall against the vertical y-axis.

For this type of graph it is easier to use graph paper, and of course you have to get out your pencil and ruler again to produce the axes. Then you just chart the points on the graph by hand (Figure 3.19). There is nothing very difficult about this; it is just a bit time consuming, and the quality of the results depends on your skill and patience.

Remember it doesn't matter in what order you plot the points so long as you don't forget any of them. All you are trying to show is that higher values of sales are associated with higher values of advertising, month by month, whenever they occur. The cloud of points should drift upwards and to the right.

By computer

By now you can probably guess how to set about this task using your PC and spreadsheet software. The steps are:

1 Type the months (just for reference), advertising spend, and sales into three adjacent columns on your spreadsheet.
2 Now set the range of values in the 'Advertising' column as the x-range. These values will then appear along the bottom of the chart, and we would expect the monthly sales to go up as we move

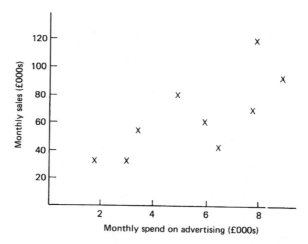

Figure 3.19   *Drawing a scatter diagram*

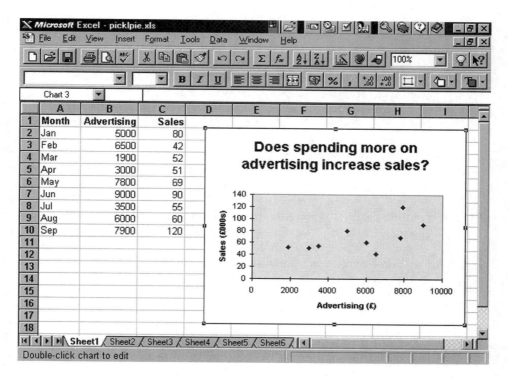

Figure 3.20   *The scatter diagram produced using Excel, ready for printing*

along the bottom axis from the lower values on the left to the higher ones on the right.

3 Similarly, set the range of values in the 'Sales' column as the *y*-range. With Chart Wizard in Excel it is just a matter of responding appropriately in the dialogue boxes.

4 The scatter graph is done, and there is a weak, positive relationship, the scatter of points revealing a trend upwards and to the
right – higher values of sales seem to be associated with higher
values of advertising. The little black squares on the border of the
chart tell you that it is selected, ready for printing, or copying and
pasting into a word processed report, for instance (Figure 3.20).

How to draw a Pareto diagram

This is a really simple technique which allows you to focus in on the
few critical factors amongst the many other important ones. There are
basically three simple steps:

● Rank items in order of value.
● Work out their proportions of the total (just as you did for the pie
chart).
● Plot a running total.

And if that is too difficult, you can even get away with just ranking
the items in order of value and plotting them as a bar chart.

Once again, the PC and spreadsheet make the task easy, at least to
produce a passable likeness to a Pareto diagram. But, first, the background: let's see where the technique came from.

Vilfredo Pareto was an Italian economist who in 1896 attempted to
show that income is not randomly distributed in any society, but that
the bulk of all income is concentrated in the hands of a fairly small
proportion of receivers. When he plotted the percentage of income
against the percentage of the population receiving the income, he
came up with a curve of characteristic shape which, as is the case
with the normal distribution curve, has since been found to crop up
in a variety of different situations. The curve is shown in Figure 3.21
and is variously known as a Pareto curve, a Lorenz curve, an 80/20
analysis and an ABC analysis.

The object of the analysis is to isolate the 'vital few' from the 'less
important many'. In the field of stock control, for instance, most factories hold a large number of small-value items and a small number of
large-value items. A simplified picture is shown in Figure 3.22, where
80 per cent of the money spent goes on only 20 per cent of the orders
placed, the rest of the orders accounting for only 20 per cent of the
expenditure. It is easy to overlook this fact, and there is a natural
tendency to spend almost as much administrative effort on small
purchase orders as on large ones. Adopting one standard form and
procedure for every purchase amounts to administrative overkill on
cheap items, while falling short on the largest non-repeating orders.

Pareto analysis can be used in any situation where you want to
focus in on the few key factors of a particular problem, from amongst
the many other rather less important factors. Here are some situations where Pareto analysis may be useful:

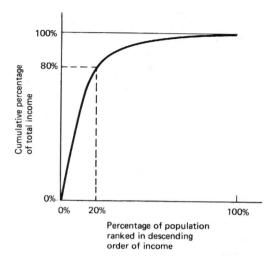

Figure 3.21   *The Pareto curve*

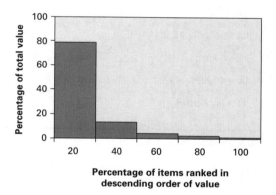

Figure 3.22   *Pareto analysis simplified*

- Cost analysis: to pick out the highest cost items, or operations, or processes, or elements.
- Time analysis: to pick out the few most time-consuming operations, or processes.
- Scrap or wastage analysis: to pick out the main causes for high scrap rates.
- Breakdown analysis: to discover the main causes for machine breakdowns.
- Quality failures: to analyse these and find where or how most of them occur.

Manually

Here is an example to see how you would do it manually. Suppose you wish to analyse the causes of downtime on a production line. The minutes lost due to each of the various causes are known, and are shown in Figure 3.23. The procedure is as follows:

Reasons for down time	Minutes lost
Tool breakages	1
Repairs	10
Operator absent	2
Low air pressure	3
Fire alarm	6
Mechanical faults	34
Electrical faults	82
Interlock open	1
Parts shortages	18
Accidents	4

Figure 3.23   *Pareto example: causes of down time and time lost*

Cause	Minutes lost	Running total	Cum. % of total
Electrical faults	82	82	51
Mechanical faults	34	116	72
Parts shortages	18	134	83
Repairs	10	144	89
Fire alarm	6	150	93
Accidents	4	154	96
Low air pressure	3	157	97
Operator absent	2	159	98
Tool breakages	1	160	99
Interlock open	1	161	100

Total minutes lost   161

Figure 3.24   *Pareto example: ranking and summing the values*

1 List the causes in order of importance, starting with the cause of most lost time, in a table with column 1 containing the causes and column 2 showing the minutes lost.
2 In column 3, list the running total of minutes lost. The last value in this column will be the total downtime.
3 In column 4, take each running total in column 3 and express it as a percentage of the total downtime (Figure 3.24).
4 Now chart the running total of percentages against the reasons listed along the bottom axis ranked in order of largest first.
5 By looking at the curve, you can now split it into two sections: the first 20 per cent of reasons (about three – electrical, mechanical, and parts – in this case) account for a little over 80 per cent of the total minutes lost, the remaining 80 per cent of reasons together accounting for only about 20 per cent of the total (Figure 3.25). If you wish, you can split the range into three sections, A, B and C. The A reasons are the most important, lying on the steep part of the curve, and the C reasons the least important, on the flat part

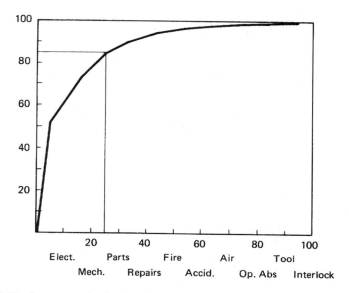

Figure 3.25   *Pareto example: drawing the curve*

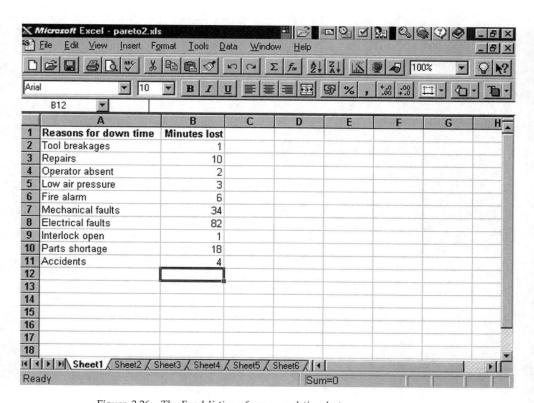

Figure 3.26   *The Excel listing of causes and time lost*

at the top. The B reasons, as you might expect, are the ones in the transitional range in between.

We now know that electrical faults are the main cause of lost time, even though it may turn out that they don't occur very often. If this is the case and we want to improve efficiency, we know where to start: by preventing even a small percentage of electrical faults we can make a big reduction in downtime.

By computer

The Excel Chart Wizard does not offer Pareto analysis, but it can be done by other means as follows:

1 List your reasons for down time in the first column of your spreadsheet.
2 Put the corresponding minutes lost in the second column (Figure 3.26).
3 Rank the items in order of descending value – in other words, largest minutes lost first, then next largest, and so on. Excel will do this for you in a flash: just use the pull-down Data menu, select

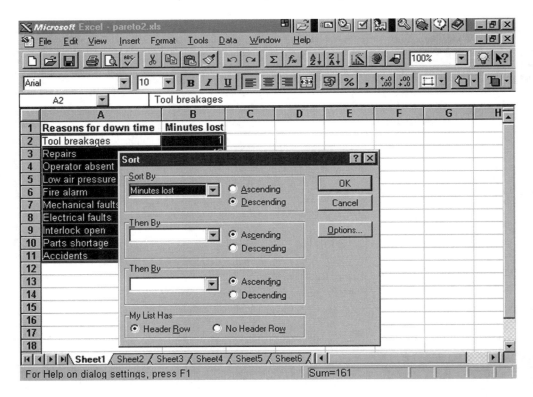

Figure 3.27 Selecting 'sort' from the 'data' menu to rank the causes in descending order

'sort', and enter the appropriate responses in the dialogue box which appears. Click on the Help button (or press the F1 key near the top left of your keyboard) for a more detailed explanation.

4 We now want to produce the running totals, so in the first row of the third column, repeat the value in the same row of column 2. Then in the next row of the third column, i.e. in cell C3, write a little formula to add the next value in column 2 to the first value in column 3. In our example using Excel, it should be = C2 + B3. This will then automatically bring the running total into cell C3. Then in one mouse operation, you can copy this formula into all the remaining cells in column 3 and the running total values will appear instantly. (Excel's Help facility explains how to copy formulae.)

5 Now in column 4 we need to display the proportions of the total that each of the values in column 3 represent. This is easy with Excel. The total at the foot of column 3 is 161 minutes, so we just take each value and divide it by 161 and multiply by 100 to show it as a percentage. In practice, one way is to put into cell D2 the following formula: = (C2/161) × 100. Then just copy this formula into the rest of the column. The proportions – percentages actually, appear instantly (Figure 3.28).

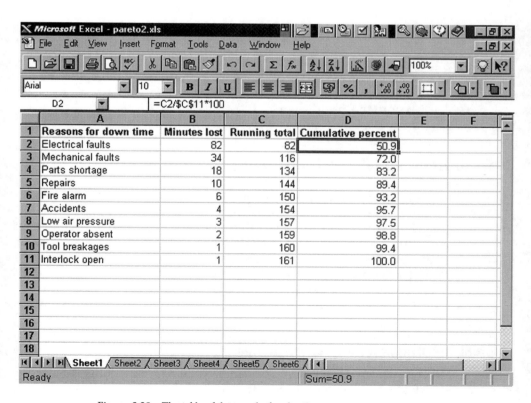

Figure 3.28 *The table of data ready for charting*

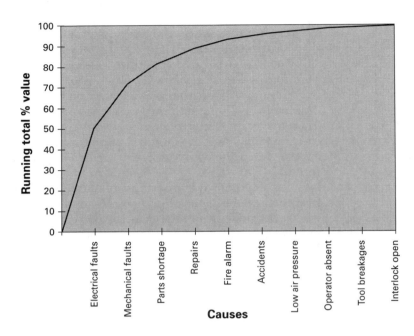

Pareto analysis of down-time

Figure 3.29   *The finished Pareto curve*

6   The final step is to display the information graphically. Use Excel's Chart Wizard to produce the appropriate combination graph (Figure 3.29). Then copy it as a picture into your word processed report and print it out.

How to draw an Ishikawa diagram

Here's another simple technique with a fancy name. In fact it is so simple you might question whether it can really be of any value. In the West we tend to undervalue simple ideas. This is certainly true of some academics who secretly feel a need to set themselves apart from lesser mortals; an idea is not worth their attention if it is easy to teach and understand. Simple but powerful ideas can sometimes be excluded from syllabuses on the grounds that they are not sufficiently intellectually demanding. Anyway this one got through the net.

A problem-solving tool for use by groups

The Ishikawa diagram is named after its originator Dr Kaoru Ishikawa, a Japanese professor who, along with Deming and Juran, was in at the beginning of Japan's quality revolution during the 1950s.

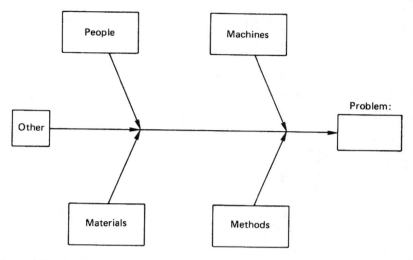

Figure 3.30   *Starting an Ishikawa diagram*

He suggested that groups called quality circles should use this diagram, also called a fishbone or cause–effect diagram, for problem solving, and identifying cause and effect relationships.

The diagram is different from some of the other techniques because it is not much use in reports and the like, for communicating information. It is more of an informal tool to provide a focus for the group, in producing a comprehensive review of all possible causes of some observed effect. It is a useful tool for a group leader working on a marker board to collect and categorize ideas.

Quality circles, or quality improvement groups as they are sometimes called, are of course concerned with the quality of a product or service. The four major categories that can have an impact on quality are humans (men), machines, materials and methods – known as the four Ms – and these usually form four of the 'bones' along with a catch-all fifth bone labelled 'other'. A generic structure for you as a group leader to use on your marker board in analysing a quality problem should look like the one shown in Figure 3.30.

You then add little bones to the five main bones for subsidiary causes under each of the five categories.

Obviously a PC is no use for preparing Ishikawa diagrams, and it is difficult even to suggest a rigid procedure for using this informal tool. Another example might help, however; Figure 3.31 shows an Ishikawa diagram produced by a quality circle while they were discussing a problem of customers in a restaurant complaining that food was cold.

The Ishikawa diagram can be used by any problem-solving group interested in determining causes and effects. It should not be reserved just for quality problems, and the main bones need not necessarily

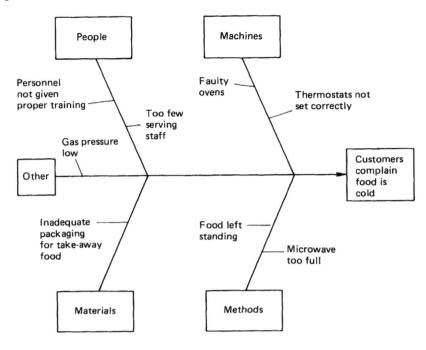

Figure 3.31 *Using the Ishikawa diagram: reviewing causes of complaint*

be just the four Ms. It can be used as an informal, flexible tool wherever appropriate.

The normal curve and standard deviation

In contrast to the earlier techniques, to get the most from this subject
you need to know some elementary statistics. We cannot go into that
here, so let's just review the main properties of the normal curve and
the way it is used.

So what is this curve? It is a bell-shaped curve which crops up in
all sorts of situations wherever variation occurs. It often arises when
we plot a frequency histogram of a scatter of results about some
central value. The histogram reveals the pattern, or profile, of the
figures, showing how much they cluster together or how widely they
spread out.

Frequency histograms

6	10	9	13	11
12	8	8	1	9
7	3	12	10	9
15	7	10	9	8

A table of data like this makes my eyes glaze over – how about you? It doesn't even help much if you know that these figures are:

● the times in minutes it took a fire brigade to arrive at the fire, or
● the weight in grams of single portion packs of jam, or
● the number of rings before a phone was answered, or
● the minutes a bus was late after its scheduled arrival time.

As we discussed earlier in this chapter, variation is undesirable because it makes for unpredictability, and customers will seek to avoid suppliers whose output of services or goods are subject to high variation.

Imagine yourself as a manager in charge of one of the situations described above, sitting at your desk studying the table of figures. You know you must control variation. What you need is to derive information from these raw data, to help you decide whether the figures are acceptable or whether you should take some kind of action.

There are three types of summarizing measure which you might find useful:

● A single typical figure – the average or mean as it should be called, or the most frequently occurring figure. You could then compare this directly with the planned schedule or target, or specification. There is usually room for improvement. The average of these figures works out at 8.85
● A single figure measure of spread. The simplest measure of spread is the range from the very smallest figure to the very largest figure in the set. It is easy to understand and to calculate – you just subtract the smallest from the largest figure. The range in this case is 14. But the range is not the best measure of spread because it is derived from just two freak figures, which is not a reliable way to describe a large body of data! As you might expect, statisticians have developed better ways to measure the spread, or variability of a set of figures. The most important of these is the standard deviation, which we will look at in more detail later. Its value in this case is 3.13. The standard deviation is always smaller than the range – usually between a quarter and a sixth of the range. It is often represented by the Greek symbol sigma, σ.
● A profile of the spread of figures. Do most of the figures cluster tightly around the average with the numbers tailing off rapidly further away? (See Figure 3.32.) Or are the figures spread more uniformly across the range? (See Figure 3.33.) In fact the distribution is roughly bell-shaped. Bar charts or histograms of the figures are one way of helping you picture exactly what is going on. Their shape can often give you important clues on what to do to improve control.

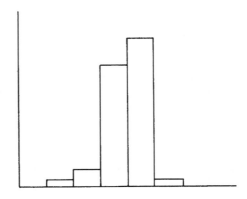

Figure 3.32   *Tightly clustered figures*

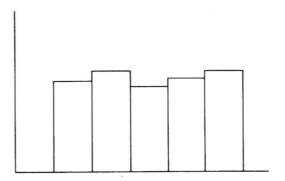

Figure 3.33   *Uniformly spread figures*

As you know by now, if your data are in digital form on disk, you can use a spreadsheet such as Excel or Lotus 1–2–3 to produce bar charts quickly and easily. Most spreadsheets also make it easy to calculate the average and standard deviation. Suppose you want to calculate them for a block of figures extending from cell A2 to cell E6 on the spreadsheet. With Excel the commands are as follows. First select the cell where you want the average to appear. Then type in the command to display the average, which is =average(A2:E6). And to display the standard deviation in another cell, just type in =stdev(A2:E6).

Alternatively, if you have a pocket calculator which can be switched to statistical or SD mode, you can key in the list of figures one after another (your user manual will describe the exact procedure), and then just press the x̄ key for the average to be displayed, and the σ key for the standard deviation to be displayed.

For decision-making, many managers feel more comfortable with just a graphical presentation, from which they can get a feel for the most commonly occurring figure, the amount and the type of spread of the figures. The table of figures we started with makes much more

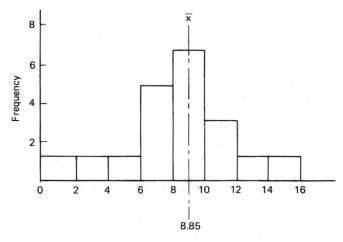

Figure 3.34   *Histogram of figures*

sense to most managers when displayed as shown in Figure 3.34. However, the single figure measures of average and standard deviation are still useful because they are more suitable for monitoring over time, to see if trends are in the right direction.

How to draw a frequency histogram

Some detail is lost when you summarize data in the form of a frequency histogram. This is because we group together values of about the same size in standard sized 'class intervals', and count how many readings there are in each class. This is how we get the hump-shaped profile, with the hump showing that most values lie close to the average. If we counted the original values, it could quite easily happen that every value would be different. There could be no hump shape then, just a region on the x-axis where the values would be more densely packed.

To get a meaningful histogram, it is important that you choose the most appropriate size for the class interval. Choose intervals that are too many and too small, and you get a histogram with lots of superfluous peaks and troughs – these are misleading because they are the product of random chance and unlikely to have any meaning. But choose too few and too large a class interval and, although you can still see the main features of the distribution, you lose too much detail and will be in danger of missing real secondary features.

As a general rule, choose a class interval which will result in a total of between four and eight classes across the full range of values. Here is a table of values that we can use as an example – they represent the mileages claimed by sales representatives over a period of weeks:

552	747	478	602	404	581	744	567
612	559	541	648	707	599	622	720
460	644	523	625	633	606	530	658
655	645	508	666	648	637	460	540
493	642	690	555	667	525	456	493
795	705	608	480	592	651	655	610
523	548	555	495	532	567	689	591
577	412	590	712	520	578	522	678

1 Search the table for the largest and smallest values. They are 404 and 795. The range is therefore 391, and this should be split into about eight classes, which will therefore have a width of $391/8 \simeq 49$. A suitable class interval to try would therefore be 50. Our x-axis should therefore extend from 401 to 800, divided up as follows: 401 to 450; 451 to 500; 501 to 550 and so on.
2 The next step is to count the number of values which fall into each of these classes. The easiest way to do this is to write down the class intervals and then, taking the readings from the table one by one, mark a tally against the appropriate class interval:

Table 2

Class	Tally
401–450	//
451–500	++++ ///
501–550	++++ ++++ /
551–600	++++ ++++ ///
601–650	++++ ++++ ////
651–700	++++ ////
701–750	++++ /
751–800	//

3 Now count the tallies, write down the frequency for each class, and check that the total of frequencies matches the total number of values in the table. You might note that the shape of the tallies actually gives you a clue as to what the histogram will actually turn out to look like – it is like a histogram turned on its side.

Table 3

Class	Tally	Frequency
401–450	//	2
451–500	++++ //	7
501–550	++++ ++++ /	11
551–600	++++ ++++ ///	13
601–650	++++ ++++ ////	14
651–700	++++ ////	9
701–750	++++ /	6
751–800	//	2
Total		64

4 Now just draw the histogram or bar chart as before (Figure 3.35). Now you can judge the average value near enough for decision-making: it is the value of the peak of the histogram – about 600. If you work it out using your calculator and the original data, the average comes to 596 to the nearest whole number.

Also the range is 800 – 400 = 400. A quarter of this is 100, and a sixth of this is 67, so we would expect the standard deviation to lie between these values. In fact, working it out with your calculator it comes to 86 to the nearest whole number. But what is the standard deviation, and why is it superior to the range as a measure of scatter?

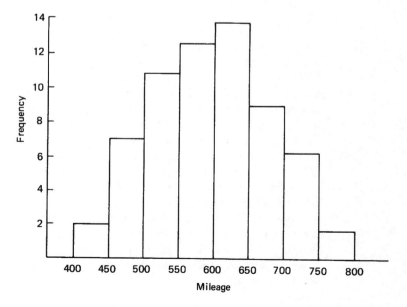

Figure 3.35 *Frequency histogram of the mileage travelled by sales representatives*

What is the standard deviation?

Like the range, it is a measure of the amount of scatter in a set of numbers. It is often represented by the Greek letter sigma, which looks like a number 6 which has fallen flat on its face, σ.

In any set of figures, it is quite common for most numbers to cluster around some value near the centre. However, we also expect some numbers to be further away from the centre. We put this down to natural variation caused by many tiny influences, some negative and some positive, which on average tend to cancel each other out but occasionally stack up to produce a value further from the centre.

This effect results in the histogram having a humped shape, but if we only know the mean of a set of figures, we have no way of knowing whether the hump is low and wide, or high and narrow. For instance you must have seen boxes of matches with the label 'Average contents 48 matches'. This could be true if some boxes were empty and some had 96 matches in. In fact most boxes contain 48 and nearly all boxes have between 47 and 49 matches, but we have to take that on trust; the average figure on its own tells us nothing about how widely spread the distribution might be.

The range is unsatisfactory for describing the spread of a whole population of figures because it is derived from just two freak figures which in themselves are far from typical. It is a bit like using a giant and a dwarf to describe the population of a country. Also, of course, the range is unsatisfactory because if the giant or the dwarf died or left, the value of the range would suddenly change – perhaps by quite a large amount.

Remember, as managers we really do need a satisfactory measure of scatter to monitor in our efforts to reduce variation. High variation is often synonymous with poor quality, and always suggests a lack of control.

The standard deviation is a much more satisfactory measure of scatter because it is derived from every value in the set of figures. The word 'deviation' is the clue: its calculation requires that we find out how far away each reading deviates from the mean. This is called the deviation of each reading (Figure 3.36).

Then what? Well, we could find the average of all the deviations. This can be done, but there are some problems here. For instance, if we just subtract the mean from each reading, we end up with about half the deviations negative for readings less than the mean, and half positive, for those greater than the mean. These then cancel each other out when we work out the average deviation; the answer always comes to zero, which is not much help.

Mathematically there are two ways round this problem. One is we could ignore the positive and negative signs and just work out the average size of the deviations. This is sometimes done and is called the mean absolute deviation (MAD), but there is a better way.

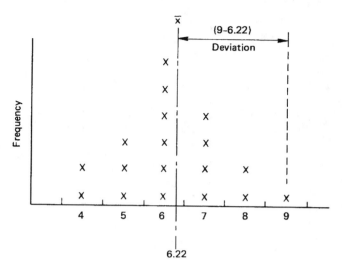

Figure 3.36   *Deviation*

You may remember from school that multiplying two negatives produces a positive. Well suppose we 'square' each of the positive and negative deviations – that is, multiply each by itself. We will then have a set of positive values for which we can calculate the average.

This mean squared deviation is more commonly known as the variance of the set of figures. But it too is not used much, mainly because it is so big and cannot be compared directly with the individual values from which it was derived. It is big because all the deviations were squared – remember? So what should we do? Unsquare it of course – that is, find the square root of the variance, or mean squared deviation. And that is exactly what the standard deviation is: the root of the mean squared deviations.

So now you know – and if you think the calculations sound tedious they certainly used to be before the calculator and the PC came galloping to the rescue. But it has always been valued because it plays a fundamental role in statistics and, of importance to managers, statistical process control (SPC). One example of SPC is the use of $\overline{X}$ charts and R charts which we will examine shortly, but first a word or two about the normal distribution.

What is a Normal distribution?

The normal distribution is a particular bell-shaped distribution (Figure 3.37), similar in shape to the frequency distribution we produced earlier from the table of mileages claimed by sales representatives. If

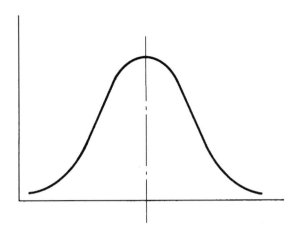

Figure 3.37 *The Normal curve*

in that example we had charted each value with a single point on the graph instead of a histogram bar, we could have drawn a curve through the points. It would have a similar bell shape to the one shown above, and we could say it approximated to the normal distribution.

In fact the Normal curve has a formula defining the shape precisely, dependent on the mean and the standard deviation. Thus for a true Normal curve, if we know the mean and the standard deviation, we know everything about that distribution. We know for instance that 95.45 per cent of all readings will lie within two standard deviations distance either side of the mean (Figure 3.38).

This is very useful because, if we have a process which we know produces a distribution that is approximately Normal in shape, we

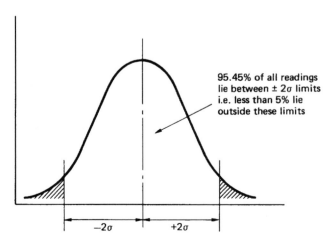

95.45% of all readings
lie between ± 2σ limits
i.e. less than 5% lie
outside these limits

-2σ $+2\sigma$

Figure 3.38 *The 4σ limits*

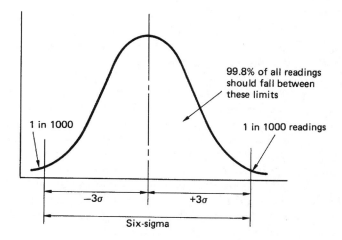

Figure 3.39   *The six-sigma limits*

can predict that about 95 per cent – that is about 19 in every 20 – of all readings in the future will lie ±2σ of the mean, so long as the process remains stable. Therefore, if we get a reading outside these limits it is a warning sign. We should begin to suspect something might have gone wrong with our process. It is sufficiently unusual for it to happen just as a result of natural variation or common causes for us to start thinking that perhaps there might be a single special cause which has upset the stability of the process to produce such a large deviation.

We also know that 99.8 per cent of all readings will lie within three standard deviations either side of the mean. These are the six-sigma limits used by IBM, Motorola and others (Figure 3.39). Again they are used to help distinguish between common and special causes of variation. They are triggers for action, because 998 in 1000 readings should lie within these limits. For a stable process the chances of a reading falling outside these limits due to expected or common cause variation is about 1 in 1000 above and 1 in 1000 below. In other words, any reading outside the 6σ limits is almost certainly due to a special cause. The process should be stopped and the cause discovered and eliminated to bring it back in control again.

So, with the Normal distribution and the standard deviation, we have the makings of a system for monitoring processes to ensure that they continue to produce within specified limits, or at least to the best they are capable of. Let us now examine how such a system can work.

X̄ and R charts

These are a proven method of monitoring and controlling a manufacturing process without the need for 100 per cent inspection. Statistical process control has been around for fifty years or more. It was during the 1940s that Walter Shewhart, an American statistician, developed the control charts which are still in use today. We can only guess how his thought processes evolved as he developed his charts, but his thinking probably went through the following phases.

To start with, he was obviously aware of the Normal distribution, its standard deviation and the chances of values lying outside the 4σ and 6σ limits. He also knew that inspection was expensive, and 100 per cent inspection adds quite a lot to the cost of each product without adding any extra value. In addition, as a statistician he would know that it is possible to infer conclusions about a whole population based upon what you find in a sample taken from that population.

He therefore probably started thinking about the process rather than the product, and whether it might be possible to control that by sampling rather than by using 100 per cent inspection to weed out the out-of-specification products. But he must also have been aware of a major difficulty, namely this. A process producing 5 per cent defective items is quite unacceptable, but is still difficult to detect by taking a single sample reading. The chance of detecting it will also be 5 per cent or a 1 in 20 chance each time. In fact we can work out that, on average, you would have to take about 15 samples before you would have an evens chance of picking up a defective item.

On the credit side, however, he would know that trends are useful in detecting and predicting change, and probably used a 'run chart' to show the output in comparison with the specification limits, and to reveal trends as a sign of change in a process (Figure 3.40). A run chart is just a continuous graph for monitoring single samples taken from the output of the process. If there is any drift or gradual change taking place then this will eventually begin to show up as a trend on the graph.

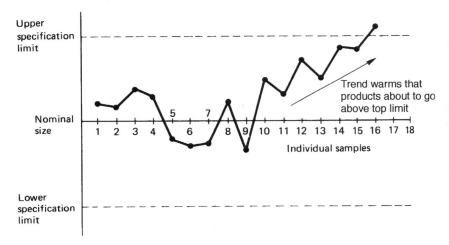

Figure 3.40   *The run chart*

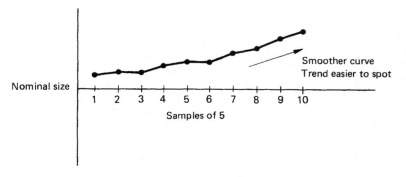

Figure 3.41 *Charting averages of samples of five*

But the masterstroke was when he tried taking small samples of five and averaging the readings, then charting the averages on a continuous graph, instead of the individual values (Figure 3.41). The sensitivity of the technique was amplified at least twenty-fold, making it very likely that an output containing only 5 per cent defective items would be detected with the very first sample of five.

So how does it work? Well, there are two effects of averaging. One effect is the random variations we expect from the process tend to be smoothed out in the averaging process. For instance, any value which is much larger than most of the output will be averaged along with four other less extreme values. Smoothing the results like this will reveal any underlying trends that might otherwise be obscured by the variation.

Another effect is that a distribution of the averages will be a normal distribution with very steep sides. If we draw in the 4σ limits for the average, we can see that only a very small change in the value of the average, $\overline{X}$, can then carry the majority of the distribution outside of the limit, indicating a very good chance that the first sample of five will have an average outside the limits, flagging a probable disturbance to the process. These 4-sigma limits for the average, $\overline{X}$, are called control limits, and are distinct from the specification limits which will be more widely set (Figure 3.42).

Don't worry if this short explanation goes over your head. The important thing to remember is that averaging samples of five and using control limits instead of specification limits amplifies the sensitivity of the monitoring process by at least twenty-fold. This makes the $\overline{X}$ chart very likely to detect an out-of-spec process at the first sample, even if it is only producing 5 per cent defective items.

Before we leave the theory to see how these charts work in practice, there is a last point to cover. By averaging samples of five, we have introduced a new problem. There is a small chance that our process may be disturbed in such a way that it starts to produce a wider scatter of results spread either side of the same average figure. For instance, if we are monitoring a filling process for filling jars to

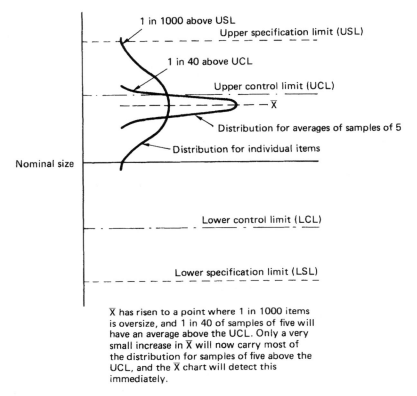

1 in 1000 above USL

Upper specification limit (USL)

1 in 40 above UCL

Upper control limit (UCL)

$-\bar{X}$

Distribution for averages of samples of 5

Distribution for individual items

Nominal size

Lower control limit (LCL)

Lower specification limit (LSL)

$\bar{X}$ has risen to a point where 1 in 1000 items is oversize, and 1 in 40 of samples of five will have an average above the UCL. Only a very small increase in $\bar{X}$ will now carry most of the distribution for samples of five above the UCL, and the $\bar{X}$ chart will detect this immediately.

Figure 3.42 *Control limits and the $\bar{X}$ chart*

a certain weight, the process could become more erratic, producing some jars that are very much overweight and some very much underweight, but in a balanced way such that the average is not affected. Our $\bar{X}$ chart will not pick this up of course, because it is only sensitive to changes in the average.

However, it is a simple matter to guard against this possibility. We produce a second chart, called an R chart, for monitoring sample range. So on taking a sample of five, we must calculate the sample average, $\bar{X}$, and plot it on the $\bar{X}$ chart, and at the same time we must calculate the sample range, R, and plot it on the R chart. The R chart has a control limit marked on it which is separate from and smaller than the overall allowable range in the whole output of the process. You would probably expect this to be the case, because the range within a sample will be smaller than the range within the overall output. After all, it would be extremely unlikely that the overall largest and overall smallest items should both be picked up within the same small sample of five.

The method of establishing the positions of the control limits on the control charts is beyond the scope of this introduction. It is,

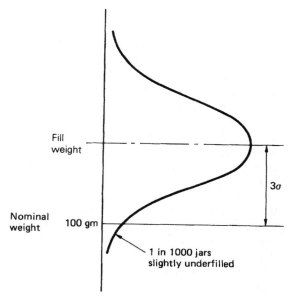

Figure 3.43   *Avoiding underfilling*

however, perfectly straightforward, and tables of factors are available to avoid the need to work out the values from first principles each time.

So let's now see how the charts are used in practice.

How to save money with $\bar{X}$ charts

Let us start by taking a look at the economics of these charts. Is it worth getting into all this statistics? I hope by now you are convinced of how important it is to reduce variation, even though the major benefits are impossible to cost-justify. But aside from that, there can also be very large and immediate direct savings to be made, by cutting down on waste.

Some time ago I used to work as a packaging engineer for General Foods, an American company now known as Kraft General Foods. One of their lines was Maxwell House instant coffee which they packed in jars on automatic filling lines running at the rate of 400 jars per minute. They employed an operator who took five jars from the line every so often, weighed the contents and plotted the results on $\bar{X}$ and R charts. We can do a few rough calculations now using estimated figures which cannot be too wide of the mark, to see if it was worth it.

How much does a 100 g jar of instant coffee retail for? Let us say £1.50, a nice round figure for the purposes of calculation. You can check in your cupboard or on the supermarket shelf: it is about right. So the coffee retails at 1.5 pence per gram.

Now, General Foods must be sure of putting at least 100 g of coffee in each jar, or they will get on the wrong side of the Weights and Measures people, so they set their filling machines to an average fill weight of slightly greater than 100 g. Then, there will be very little chance of any underfilling due to the natural variation in fill weight produced by the filler. Ideally, the filler should be set to fill at an average fill weight of just 3σ above the nominal fill weight as shown in Figure 3.43.

In theory this will result in about one jar in 1000 being very slightly underfilled, which in practice is as good as can be expected. To achieve a consistent average fill weight at this setting, however, requires constant monitoring using control charts as outlined above.

Now suppose this approach saves, on average, just 1 g of instant coffee per jar – far less than a teaspoon full – just a few grains on the end of your spoon. How much money will be saved in a year? For 400 jars per minute over an 8-hour shift the saving is

$400 \times 60 \times 8 = 192,000$ jars

Over five days a week for a year this grows to

$192,000 \times 5 \times 50 = 48$ million jars

The retail value in pounds for 1 g from each jar is

$48,000,000 \times 1.5/100 = £720,000$

Now let us take just one-tenth of this as the true figure, to take account of the retail mark-up, and lost production due to breakdowns and market restrictions. £72,000 would be enough to pay for the running of the control charts and still leave a saving of £1000 per week. Not bad, eh? And that's just on one of many packing lines in the factory. It's amazing how those few grains from each jar add up, isn't it.

The charts have to be set up in advance by someone with the know-how to do it. Then anyone can fill in the charts and know what to do if the charts flag a warning. These are the steps:

1 Run the process for a while until it settles down. Then take about ten samples of five, making fifty in all. Calculate the averages and ranges of these samples and then look up in the appropriate tables for the positions of the control limits to set on the charts.

2 Now give the charts to the operators and tell them how often to take samples. This will depend on the value of the product, the rate of production, and the costs of sampling. If a sample shows that the process has gone out of control, then all the output since the previous sample may have to be re-processed. The sampling should therefore be fairly frequent. But if the sampling involves the destruction of the product, then sampling should not be too frequent.

3 The operators should then take samples at the recommended intervals, and if the $\overline{X}$ and the R plot satisfactorily within the control limits, they should allow the process to continue without adjustment.

4 If, however, an $\overline{X}$ value falls outside the 2σ limits, this is a warning that the process may have gone out of control or is on the point of going out of control. However, even when the process is in

control, the 2σ limits will still only contain nineteen out of every twenty values, and one in forty readings should be expected to fall above the limit, and one in forty below. The rule is, therefore, that if there is no trend leading up to the out-of-limit value, the process should be allowed to continue without adjustment, but another sample of five should be taken immediately.

5 If this too falls outside the limit, the process should be stopped and reset, because with the process still in control the chance of two out-of-limit values occurring consecutively is $1/40 \times 1/40$ or one in 1600. This is such a remote chance, that we must conclude that normal variation is not the cause and there is some other special cause for the two out-of-limit values, which must be determined and eliminated to bring the process back into control.

I hope you can see now that control charts are a very powerful way of distinguishing between common and special causes of variation. If you are ever in charge of a process that you think may benefit from their application, you can find out more about them from the references given at the end of this chapter.

Competence self-assessment

We have covered a lot of ground in this chapter. We have touched on a variety of different techniques – all of direct relevance to managers – which are easy enough to read about, but it is not until you try using them yourself that you discover whether you truly understand how to use them.

If you haven't used some of these techniques before, try the following exercises. You can do some of them manually or using a PC, whichever you prefer. Either way, it can only add to your confidence and repertoire of management skills.

Pie charts and bar charts

1 In the 1992 Microsoft/BIM survey of UK managers, when asked how important information technology (IT) is to their jobs, managers responded as follows:

Importance of IT to job	Per cent
Fundamental to your job	34
Important to your job	41
Supports job in the background	19
Largely peripheral to your job	4
Don't know	2
	100

Draw a pie chart to represent these data.

2 Recent mortality statistics produced for Oxfordshire Health Authority analysed causes of death under ninety different headings. In summary, there were 4681 deaths, of which 1255 were caused by neoplasm, 2134 were caused by circulatory diseases, and the rest by a variety of other causes. Show these data as a pie chart, and add a suitable title.

3 In the 1992 Microsoft/BIM survey, British managers were asked what types of job they used IT for. They responded as follows:

Type of job	Per cent
Producing documents	53
Planning/forecasting/budgeting	46
Monitoring/reviewing performance	44
Communicating with others	14
Other jobs	3

Represent these data as a bar chart, suitably annotated and titled.

4 For the year ended 31 December 1995, British Gas plc reported current assets as follows:

	£ (millions)
Stocks	309
Debtors	3180
Cash at bank and in hand	1309
Total	4798

Show this as a bar chart. Also it show as a pie chart. Which do you think is the most effective as a communication?

Scatter diagrams

5 Plot a scatter diagram for the following small (too small to be representative) sample, to see if there is any relationship between price and maximum speed in small cars. The data were derived from What Car? magazine, August 1996.

Model	Price (£)	Max. speed (mph)
Alfa Romeo 145, 1.6	12,029	114
BMW 316I Compact	14,120	121
Fiat Cinquecento	6,022	82
Lada Riva 1500E	4,895	95
Nissan Micra 1.0 Shape	7,660	89
Proton 1.3 GL	7,599	96
Renault Clio 1.2 RL	7,988	96
Rover Mini Mayfair	7,946	87
Toyota Starlet 1.3 Sportif	8,044	103

Number the cars 1 to 9 and mark each point on the graph with the appropriate reference number.

6 Texmills DIY wants to see if sales are boosted by newspaper advertising. The level of advertising, and the volume of sales for each of seven months are as follows:

Month	Advertising spend (£)	Sales volume (£)
June	8,630	102,430
July	4,480	103,720
August	19,110	151,220
September	12,160	148,990
October	3,910	53,100
November	8,470	68,800
December	17,140	118,750

Chart these data as a scatter diagram. What does the diagram indicate?

Pareto analysis

7 The stores in a hospital department holds just ten items in stock. The usage and values of the items are as follows:

Item	Annual usage (items)	Unit value (£)
1	244	68.10
2	585	58.30
3	76	76.35
4	74	52.64
5	7,413	4.60
6	63,800	3.21
7	2,135	2.95
8	558	4.30
9	424	9.20
10	468	13.45

Calculate the value of annual usage for each item. Rank them in descending order, and plot them as a Pareto curve.

Which approximately 20 per cent of the items form approximately 80 per cent of the annual usage value? Which items would you classify as A, B and C items?

---

8 There are ten products in the range offered by a marketing company. The sales revenue attributable to each product is as follows:

Product ref.	Sales revenue (£000)
1	310
2	140
3	44
4	180
5	86
6	1,067
7	116
8	96
9	68
10	720

Set these products on a Pareto curve, and thus identify the few vital products from amongst the many other important products.

Cause–effect diagrams

9 An airline operating out of Heathrow has a problem of late flight departures. A quality group is convened to uncover the causes of late departure. During a meeting of the group, the main reasons suggested by members were as follows:

- Aircraft arrival delayed.
- Cockpit crew late or unavailable.
- Aircraft problem requiring maintenance.
- Late on-board catering supplies.
- Slow security clearance procedures.
- Pushback tug unavailable when required.
- Baggage handlers late to aircraft.
- Fuel late to aircraft.
- Air traffic control delays.
- Cabin cleaners late.
- Delays due to bad weather.
- Flight weight and balance sheet late.
- Delay for late passengers.
- Cabin crews late.

Prepare a cause–effect (Ishikawa) diagram with bones for the four Ms and 'Other' causes. Fill in the effect on the right-hand side, then attach the causes listed above to the appropriate bones.

10 Write down in two or three words a problem or undesirable effect you are aware of at work. Construct a fishbone diagram consisting of the four Ms and any other bones necessary, and then attach possible causes to the appropriate bones. If possible, discuss the diagram with someone else familiar with the problem, and see if together you can add to the possible causes.

Histograms

11 A fruit farmer harvests cooking apples from his trees. The weights of apples in kilograms yielded by each of thirty trees is shown below:

41.3	52.6	58.9	49.3	53.6
66.8	46.3	51.3	54.4	65.1
45.8	62.3	42.3	46.8	48.8
48.7	51.7	48.3	56.2	53.2
54.1	64.7	63.8	47.2	64.6
46.1	57.5	49.4	65.2	59.3

Produce a frequency histogram of these data, using a class interval of 5 kg.

From the histogram, estimate the average weight of apples produced per tree. Compare this value with the true mean of the above figures, computed using your PC or calculator.

Divide the range by 4. This should give you a rough estimate of the standard deviation. Compute the standard deviation, using your calculator or PC, from the table of figures above. How does it compare with the estimate?

Would you say the histogram has a shape which approximates to the normal curve?

12 A company makes drinking chocolate as a powder to be made up with hot milk. The company packs it for sale in containers marked 250 g. The filler delivers a measured volume of the powder, which because of variations in the density of the powder results in a small amount of variation in fill weight. The contents of 1000 successive packs were weighed, and the results are shown in the table below.

Weight (g)	Frequency
Over 250.0, up to 250.5	5
Over 250.5, up to 251.0	17
Over 251.0, up to 251.5	44
Over 251.5, up to 252.0	92
Over 252.0, up to 252.5	150
Over 252.5, up to 253.0	192
Over 253.0, up to 253.5	192
Over 253.5, up to 254.0	150
Over 254.0, up to 254.5	92
Over 254.5, up to 255.0	44
Over 255.0, up to 255.5	17
Over 255.5, up to 256.0	5

Produce a frequency histogram of these figures. Draw in the nominal container weight. Estimate the average fill weight being produced by the filler. Should the filler be adjusted to another average fill weight?

Does this histogram approximate in shape to the normal curve? If so, why might this be worth knowing?

References and further reading

Caplen, R. H. (1988). *A Practical Approach to Quality Control*. Hutchinson.
Curwin, J. and Slater, R. (1996). *Quantitative Methods for Business Decisions*. (4th edition). Chapman and Hall.

4 Computers, programs and communications

Why is this chapter relevant?

Computers are business machines: they are as relevant to business advantage today as the telephone and typewriter when they were first used in the era of the carrier pigeon. There is a difference though. The computer is more complex than the phone or typewriter, and it is not so immediately obvious how to use it for business advantage.

Does it matter that some managers don't know much about how their business machines work? You don't need to know what goes on under the bonnet when you drive your car to the supermarket or pick up the kids from school. But professional users should know more about their machines than casual users. You can be sure that Damon Hill knows a lot about engines, gearboxes, differentials and brake systems. Extensive knowledge can be crucial, especially in today's competitive business environment.

Computers are changing our jobs as managers:

● We can use them to reach out through networks to find the information we need, and to communicate more freely with customers, colleagues and suppliers.
● We can make better decisions by modelling and forecasting, and we can understand situations better through 'what-if' analysis.
● We can store virtually unlimited numbers of files – and find any one of them in seconds.

Professional users need to know more than just how to drive their machines: when the going gets tough, those that do will come through in better shape.

'Managers scared of computers'

This headline appeared in 1992 on the front page of *Management News*, the newspaper of the Institute of Management (IM). The article described the results of a survey of IM members carried out jointly by Microsoft and IM, which showed that 92 per cent of managers felt uncomfortable with computer technology. But computers are much more user-friendly now, and if the survey were to be repeated today the results would be different – yet I suspect many managers still don't exploit their computers fully. Why should this be? Broadly because of cultural and ability barriers.

The cultural barrier is a hangover from our recent industrial past. In those days there was a deep divide between managers and workers, and managers did not operate machines. That was for craftsmen on the shop floor, and women typists in the office. Some managers still associate computers – and especially keyboards – with the low status of craftsmen and typists. This is a crippling, out-dated attitude for any manager to have in the information age. Such managers are being swept away by business re-engineering programmes, or simply being replaced by someone from the raft of new young managers who were born into homes with personal computers (PCs), and use them as naturally as the phone.

The ability barriers are more excusable – reflecting perhaps choices made at school, or our natural predisposition. Everyone has some knowledge gaps which it is now too late to own up to. Can you construct a simple formula, or calculate a percentage? How's your English grammar and vocabulary? And are you a single-finger 'hunt and peck' typist? These shortcomings are common human failings, but they can be put right. You can't expect to make beautiful music without learning the tunes and practising your scales.

Pharmaco sales reps re-deploy as self-managing teams with laptops

Jackie Barlow was 18 years old when she started as a lab technician at Pharmaco's London plant. She soon transferred to the buyer's office, and then moved into the field as a representative in the Trent region. Today she has 15 years experience with the company, and looks after between 20 and 30 customers who place about £1 million worth of business each year. Jackie has seen big changes recently in the way sales and marketing information is handled by the company.

In 1990, each representative reported to an area manager, and kept in touch by attending regional sales meetings, also by submitting regular hand-written reports and using the phone for urgent messages. Jackie's field intelligence reports went first to her area manager who would annotate them before sending them to Head Office. In this paper-based bureaucracy typical of the period, Jackie kept her own personal records of customers and potential customers on standard record sheets which the area manager would inspect from time to time. Keeping in touch and handling information was slow, labour intensive and left less time for meeting the customers.

Today Jackie and her colleagues in the Trent region use Compaq laptop computers to communicate and maintain records, and their self-esteem is enhanced as they take control of their work and perform more effectively as a team. Jackie never needs to visit Pharmaco's London office, except for training courses, as the free flow of up-to-date information between the 30 representatives in her region is allowing them increasingly to manage their own affairs. They operate as four subgroups specializing in drugs for particular medical conditions: asthma, gastro-intestinal complaints, etc.

Before the day's visits, Jackie looks through the customer files stored on her laptop, to review details of the last visit and the objectives she had set for the next call. In her car after each visit she updates the records on her laptop, and then at the end of the day she plugs her laptop into a telephone socket and runs a software package which logs on to Pharmaco's mainframe computer in London. The software first transfers the updated records onto the company database, then waits for the mainframe to call back. Some time during the night after uploading the new data from all the reps, the mainframe then downloads the up-dated customer files back onto all the laptops. Thus, before visiting a customer, Jackie always has the latest details of visits made by reps from other subgroups.

Most of the time Jackie is on her own or with customers. She keeps in touch with her team by car phone, voice mail and home answerphone. Team members also use their laptops and Microsoft Works to prepare memos, which are then exchanged when logged on to the mainframe in the evenings. They will always need to meet from time to time, but meetings can be called by anyone and are held in the field at a convenient hotel, with members fitting in their visits around it, to make the best use of time.

The inefficient bureaucratic days of command-and-control are slipping away, though for the time being Pharmaco still appoint a business manager for each region who is responsible for delivering the business to the company. Moving to full self-management may take a few more years, but the benefits to the team and the company are obvious.

'It's much more of a living situation than anything hierarchical', says Jackie. 'We're moving to a situation where any team member feels empowered to play a full part in influencing the team's performance.'

(This case study outlines developments in a real international pharmaceutical company. However, for business reasons the names used are fictitious.)

In 1992, about three-quarters of managers actually used computers, but nearly all (92 per cent) felt uncomfortable with the technology! The survey suggests that managers then were not adequately trained in the technology. Few managers then felt they got adequate time, training and support to develop the necessary skills. Most were left to pick up what they could from colleagues at work. By how much have things improved today?

Even in 1992 managers were convinced of the importance of computers to their jobs – yet they felt that computers were not used as well as they could be. Only 9 per cent used computers to share information with their colleagues, and 53 per cent used PCs most frequently as glorified typewriters to produce documents.

These results painted a rather disturbing picture. You can read a fuller account of the survey in *Management Today*, February 1992 issue, but the main observations were that most managers used PCs mainly to edit documents – an inappropriate use of senior management time. And the reasons managers quoted for not applying computers in more imaginative ways? The main ones quoted were:

- The time it took to master systems.
- Lack of training and technical support.
- Use of jargon.

I expect some of these conclusions may still ring a few bells for you, although with the rapid adoption of Internet technology (networking and multimedia) by business, the use of computers for team working, networking and teleworking must be more common today. However, there are still many organizations where managers just don't see their promotion prospects depending on how widely and imaginatively they use computers. If they did, they would take the time, get the training, insist on the technical support and learn the jargon. Does your chief executive say 'Get your report printed and circulated by Friday and we'll discuss it at next week's meeting'. Or does she/he say 'Circulate your report on the network, arrange a computer conference for tomorrow and we'll decide then'? As with most things, we all take our lead from the chief executive – often an older technophobe – and hence our reluctance to change. We will never all work in paperless offices, although some of the methods may arrive sooner than we think.

Computers used to be inflexible. They wouldn't allow us to work with them in our old informal ways: for instance we felt we didn't 'own' our copy of a report on screen. However, some systems now allow users to highlight passages, make notes in the margin, and compare two pages at the same time, and this is a big help. But, even so, we should not expect computers to replace completely the older media such as paper and phones: we should expect to find it more appropriate to use computers in some cases, and paper or the phone in others. So printer makers needn't worry – we're always going to need some printouts, although paperwork for internal circulation seems destined to decline. Cumbersome printing and manual delivery is just not fast enough now. The accelerating pace of business means that, in order to keep up, immediate easy access to information is now essential.

Jargon

Managers claim that the jargon makes it difficult to learn about computers, and you probably understand why. Have you ever felt excluded from discussion and vaguely guilty because you don't know for instance what RAM is, or resentful even because you suspect the computer people are exploiting the situation? But all specialists use jargon, and computer people are no worse than accountants with their 'internal rates of return' and 'quick ratios'.

Jargon performs a useful function, making it much easier for those in the know to discuss difficult, but commonly occurring, concepts. Take the word 'offside' in football for instance. Think how difficult it would be for a radio sports commentator if forbidden to use the word offside for fear of excluding some listeners. Or ask a lawyer what a 'contract' is, and you'll be treated to a lecture. Every professional or special interest group has its own jargon and you can probably think of examples in photography, motor sport, knitting and hi-fi, as well as computers. Magazines serving these special interests often have a beginners page devoted to explaining week by week different jargon terms – a kind of extended glossary. Magazine publishers know that jargon can exclude newcomers, but it can also act as a pointer to areas of knowledge which newcomers need to acquire if they are to understand reports or join in any meaningful debate on the subject. So in the best popular magazine tradition, let us also start by busting six key jargon terms:

- Hardware.
- Software.
- Memory.
- Printouts.
- Networks.
- Multimedia.

Hardware

If it is part of a computer system and you can switch it on, it is hardware. Hardware forms part of most business information systems, and when you use it, you and the hardware together form the human–computer interface, across which data and information are exchanged. You can add information to the system using an input device – usually a keyboard – and you can receive information from the system in the form of a display on a screen, or a printout from a printer. These are the usual computer output devices.

Business information systems usually consist of a number of computers all linked together to form a communications network, with information able to flow through the network from one computer to another. If you work in an organization which has such a system, then the computer on your desk can be thought of as a subsystem, just part of the whole information system.

What is a system? All systems have inputs, storage, processes and outputs. For instance your hot water system at home has cold water and fuel as the main inputs. The heating of the water in the boiler is the process, and the hot water may be stored in the cylinder before being drawn off as output in the bathroom and kitchen.

Similarly, a business information system has inputs of data which can be stored in various ways before being processed into information which can be drawn off by users wherever it is needed. The same is true of the subsystem – the computer on your desk. It too has inputs, storage, processes and outputs.

We are getting deep into jargon country with output devices alone quite capable of filling several pages with technical terms. We will return to these later and move on now to software.

Software

In contrast to hardware which is solid and permanent, software consists of programs, which are lists of instructions for the computer to carry out. Like telephone messages they are intangible and impermanent, and can be sent via cables, telephone lines and satellite transmissions. Software exists as binary code, a series of pulses switching on and off – rather like the dots and dashes of Morse code, to which computers can respond.

A computer program starts its life by being typed by a programmer into a computer as a set of instructions called a file. Each file is designed to get the computer to perform a particular function and, when first typed in, exists only in the computer's main memory circuits and would be lost if the computer were switched off. Programmers therefore take copies of their work by recording each new file onto a disk which can be played back if necessary, to re-load the program into the computer. The disks are made of magnetic material rather like that used for audio and video tapes, and the code is saved as a series of microscopic magnetized spots and spaces. There is much more to learn about software, but in this brief introduction we have now reached an appropriate point to turn to the next jargon term.

Memory

If you have ever heard computer buffs talking about Kay and Meg, don't get the wrong idea. They are not talking about two popular girls in the Computer Department – they are just referring to the size of computer files or memory chips. 500kb (pronounced 500 'kay') means 500 kilobytes, and 2Mb (pronounced 2 'meg') means 2 megabytes. Kilo means one thousand, and mega means one million, so 500kb is the same as half a megabyte.

So what is a byte? Simple – a byte is eight bits. And a bit? This is a contraction of the term binary digit, which exists as the presence (or absence) of a magnetized spot on a disk, or the presence (or absence) of a signal pulse travelling down a wire. Up to eight bits are needed to code each of the 52 alphabetic characters (including upper and lower case), the 10 numeric characters, and the other punctuation and special characters used by computers. So the number of bytes of memory is the number of characters that can be stored. Typically, a single page of text from a report may take up about 2kb of space in the main memory of a computer. Main memory is usually referred to as RAM, standing for random access memory, because the computer can go straight to any part of a file without having to search from the beginning – as would be the case if the file had been recorded onto tape. The amount of RAM a computer has is an important indicator of its power and capacity – rather like engine size in cars. In 1996, a typical new PC would be fitted with 8Mb or 16Mb of RAM, but this typical figure tends to double every year or two.

There are many other forms of storage which we will return to later.

Printouts

Computer printouts can be that concertina-fold paper with the holes down the side and green horizontal stripes which make your eyes glaze over – or it can be crisp white pages with clear diagrams and elegant text that looks just like it has been typeset.

Until recently most computer printers were direct descendants of the typewriter, striking metal characters one after the other through an inked ribbon onto the paper, and printing a line of text at a time. The expansion in the use of PCs, however, brought a demand for cheaper printers – including ones which could handle images as well as text. The dot-matrix printer became very popular, capable of producing a wide range of different alphanumeric characters, and images too. Instead of using many different metal characters, the dot matrix uses a single print head and builds up characters and images from dots created by needles struck through an inked ribbon. A typical print head has 24 needles arranged in a six by four rectangle, from which each character can be constructed. For instance, a simple capital 'L' would only require the needles in the bottom row and left column (Figure 4.1).

Images can also be constructed by 'bit-mapping', i.e. producing a picture from thousands of dots. The picture is broken down into

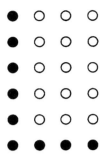

Figure 4.1 *A dot-matrix letter 'L'*

columns and rows of tiny picture cells or pixels, and the needles in the print head are fired by bits of data in one of the two binary states, fed to the printer by the computer.

Dot-matrix printers are cheap and versatile, but the print quality is often poor (draft quality), though quite good results can be achieved by changing the ribbon regularly and getting the printer to strike more than once over each line of text (near-laser quality, or NLQ). Dot-matrix printers are also noisy, and in a busy office they need to be put in a sound-proofed cabinet.

The latest types of printer are the ink-jet and the laser. The ink-jet printer works on the same principle as the dot matrix, but instead of using needles it fires microscopic jets of ink onto the paper to produce the bit-mapped characters and images. The laser, on the other hand, owes more to the photocopier than the typewriter. A needle-sharp laser beam scans the surface of a printing drum to create a pattern of electrostatic charge. Toner powder is attracted to the charged areas, then transferred to the paper and melted on. Laser printers are more expensive but are fast and produce excellent quality. Ink-jet printers are cheaper but still produce very good results. Both types of printer are quiet in use.

Printed output is often referred to as hard copy output because, like hardware, it is fixed and difficult to change. Other forms of output are much easier to change, edit and develop. For instance, output to disk or through a network.

Networks

Suppose your colleague has typed a joint report and you need to check it through. She could print a draft copy and pass it to you for marking up. Then you could pass it back and she could edit the original on her disk before printing again. Should you check it again before it is replicated and circulated?

Alternatively, the first draft produced by your colleague could be transferred electronically to your screen by exchanging disks, or better still through a network connection. You could scan through it making corrections on screen as you go, then send the edited version back to your colleague's computer for her to print, replicate and circulate.

Networks – great for team working like this – come in two forms: LANs, or local area networks, which serve a single site, often a single room; and WANs, or wide area networks, which can extend world-wide.

LANs are fast. They sometimes use 'parallel' communications between computers, with eight or more wires so that the eight bits of a byte can all be sent down the network at the same time, each along its own wire. WANs, however, mostly use 'serial' connections, a coaxial cable or a twisted pair carrying bits as pulses following each other one at a time down the same single wire.

Often it is impractical to have special lines laid just for the network, and some links may be established through the communications services of bulk carriers such as British Telecom, Mercury and others. Telephone networks though, are designed to carry voice messages and sounds, not the binary voltage pulses that computers use, and so a special piece of gear called a modem is used to convert the pulses into sounds when sending messages into the telephone network, and to convert sounds back into computer code when receiving. Modem is short for modulator–demodulator, and its circuitry can be installed as a separate box between the computer and the telephone socket, or as a circuit board or 'card' mounted in one of the spare slots actually inside the PC main unit.

Of course the mother of all networks is the Internet, which you cannot fail to have heard about, despite its origins as a communications network for university scientists and defence researchers in the USA. When it was invented in 1969 it could only handle text and numbers in monochrome, and demanded programming skills with the Unix operating system. Now, however, it handles not only text, but also images, video clips and hi-fi sound – in other words, multi-media. Also, some very clever user interface programs such as Netscape, and Internet Explorer have been devised, which make it possible for almost anyone to browse through – or 'surf' – the Internet by calling up and reading pages of information held at remote sites all around the world. The home page of UCLA shown in Figure 4.2 took less than 20 seconds to appear on my screen – fetched from Los Angeles, 6000 miles away on the Pacific coast of America.

The Internet is a strange phenomenon arising from the almost zero marginal cost of digital information (the cost of sending one extra message) – a point raised briefly at the beginning of Chapter 2. It works like this: to fulfil their role, universities must have computers and the permanently rented land lines which connect them, so all the fixed costs have already been met. Thus once the hardware is installed, the only direct cost of sending a message is the tiny unmeasured amount of electricity used to form the digital pulses of the message. The messages are in effect free, unless in total they begin to fill the bandwidth, forcing extra hardware to be purchased.

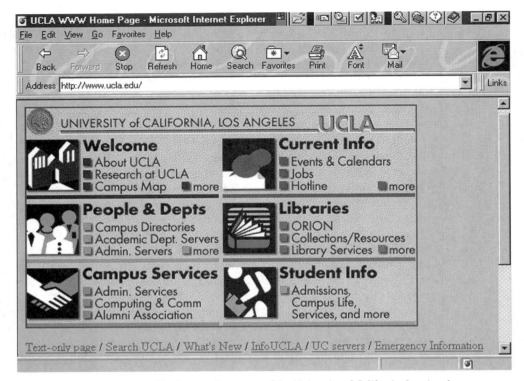

Figure 4.2   *The Internet home page of the University of California, Los Angeles*

In the 1980s, commercial organizations were allowed access to the university research network, and now the big network service providers such as CompuServe, America On Line, and Microsoft Net all offer connections to the Internet. This enormous integrated network extends throughout the world, wherever there is a telephone service. And connecting to another site anywhere in the world usually takes just minutes, and costs just pennies. From your home PC in the UK you can send a ten page report to a colleague in Australia and it gets there almost instantaneously. Or you can visit the site of the University of Chicago and see what courses they offer – and all for the price of a local telephone call to your service provider's access point.

Multimedia

The word multimedia may well fall into disuse soon. It is fashionable now because we are still a little amazed at the new capabilities which computers have recently acquired. Just a few years ago, computers could only produce silent displays of text and numbers, except for the occasional 'beep' when we hit a wrong key. Now our PCs deliver long video clips of almost TV quality, accompanied by high-fidelity stereo sound. Good examples of multimedia of this type are the CD-ROM encyclopaedias, such as *Encarta* from Microsoft, and the *Grolier* encyclopaedia. Soon, maybe, nearly all computers and software will be multimedia, and then we will no longer have any need for the word.

Using software

Hardware is the machinery and software is the lists of instructions which drives the machinery to automate routine office work. So far we have concentrated on the smaller computer known as the PC or personal computer, because they are so common nowadays, yet it is built from similar components to those used for the larger machines known as mainframes. We will leave the bigger computers until the next chapter. The PC is complicated enough to start with; it is so complex even expert users don't profess to know everything. No single person can know everything there is to know about how the PC works: the further you dig down into the detailed design the more specialized it becomes.

Fortunately, though, you only need to learn a bit about the basics to develop an instinct for what should be possible. Then it just boils down to finding out how to invoke the appropriate routines. Also, as time goes by and computers develop, it is becoming more and more possible to use the PC without knowing anything about its workings. You can use the mouse for inputs, the screen for output, and regard the system in between as a mysterious 'black box'. But, occasionally, to save time or to avoid effort, you may want to try something out of the ordinary, such as copying data to a colleague or customer, and without knowing something about the workings you won't even know if it is possible.

There are three main reasons why managing information electronically is superior to manual methods:

- Speed of access: you can search with blinding speed in order to find particular facts or figures.
- Ease of editing: you can change information with supreme ease by adding, changing or deleting it.
- Ease of saving: you can copy and store information freely and instantly.

For instance, you can take out a file, use it or change it, then put it back again fast and easily, even if you have many thousands of files.

This all probably sounds too general to strike much of a chord with you, so let us take a look at how these three processes of accessing, editing and saving actually work with real information and real software. Well, information comes in three main forms:

- Text or words.
- Numbers and formulae.
- Graphics or images.

Different software packages are designed to handle each of these. For instance, if you work with text, you should use word-processing software, whereas for numbers you should perhaps choose a spreadsheet package. For technical drawings, computer-aided design software might be appropriate. Each of these types of package are excellent when working with the main form of information for which they were designed, but only have limited capacity for handling the other two forms. However, the processes of accessing, editing and saving work just the same, whatever the software package and form of information being used.

Seeing as more word processing is done on PCs than any other task, let us use that to illustrate the principles. Then we can see how exactly the same principles apply to spreadsheets. And finally we will do a round-up of the other packages to see how the principles apply there too.

Word processing

All work produced on PCs is held in files. A file can be as short as a single-line memo, or as long as the chapter of a book. Most word-processed files are just a few pages long, which at 2 or 3kb per page means most files are probably about 2–10kb in size.

Accessing

With your PC you can pull out and view a file in seconds at the click of a mouse, or by pressing a few keys, whereas viewing paper files involves getting up from your desk and walking to the filing cabinets, finding the right drawer, thumbing across the names, etc. Of course you need to know the file name, and the ease of accessing a particular file depends in both cases on how the files are named and organized. We will discuss file organization later, as it applies to all files, not just word-processed ones. But, even if you don't know the name of the file you are seeking, you should still be able to find it fairly quickly. If you can think of any unique word which appears in the file you want, you can ask your PC to search all your files for that key word. The PC will then display a list of file names, indicating which files, if any, contain the key word.

Figure 4.3 shows the dialogue box which appears when you select File-Open, working with Microsoft Word 7.0. I can't remember which file I want to open, but I know the word 'personnel' is used in it, so I type PERSONNEL in the Text or property box, and then

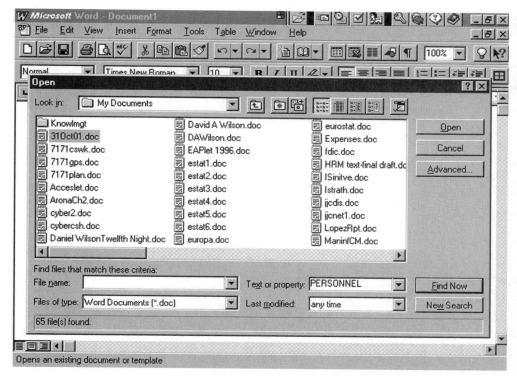

Figure 4.3   *The File-Open dialogue box in Microsoft Word 7.0*

click on the Find Now button. All the files listed in the dialogue box disappear except for three, all of which contain the word 'personnel' (see Figure 4.4).

A simple double-click on one of them is all that is needed to open the file. This is a really useful feature, especially when you have a list of hundreds of files, and you can think of a unique word in the text – perhaps a person's name for instance. Most modern word processors offer a similar feature.

Editing

This is the process which is so easy with a computer that it makes possible completely new ways of working with information. Information on paper is difficult to change. Consider, for instance, a sales letter produced on a conventional typewriter. Any typographical errors usually require the whole letter to be retyped, during which there is always the possibility that further typos will be introduced. With typewriter technology, perfection was difficult to achieve. It depended upon well-trained and conscientious secretarial staff.

The word processor has changed all that by making it possible to store electronically the sequence of key strokes made by the typist. The sequence is displayed on screen as it would appear on paper and

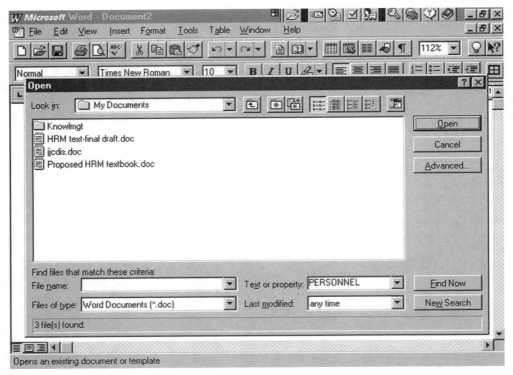

Figure 4.4 *Word 7.0 finds three files containing the word 'Personnel'*

any changes are simple to make. Words can be inserted or deleted and the text following the change moves across to accommodate the change. If there are then too many or too few words to fit on that line, words automatically roll over or back to just fill the line where the change was made, and all subsequent lines are adjusted as well.

When you have got the sales letter appearing on screen just how you want it, you can print it.

If later you want a different version of the letter, printed between narrower margins, or in a different typeface, it is a piece of cake to do. No need to re-key all the words – the same long string of keystrokes stored in memory or on disk can simply be set to print in the new format. Also 'cut and paste' operations are simple to do electronically. Suppose you want to start the letter with a sentence which is in the middle of the letter at present. No problem. Select the required block of text and indicate where you want it moved to and the computer will do the rest.

Also, in just the same way you can take a block of text from one file and insert it anywhere in another. This facility opens up new possibilities and accounts for the huge growth in junk mail we receive now. It becomes possible for sales letters to be tailored to the circumstances of each reader. In the days of the typewriter, mailing shots used to be Xeroxed or printed, with the space for the name and address left blank for a typist to fill later. It was obvious to the reader, and the letters also had to be couched in very general terms to cover a wide range of reader circumstances. The readers could see they were being batch processed: not very flattering and, as a consequence, not very effective as a sales pitch. Now with a word processor and a little ingenuity, the same process can be performed, but with results that look like they have been typed individually for each reader. The bulk of the letter can still be standard, with spaces left for the operator to fill in personal comments based on knowledge of the particular reader.

The direct mail organizations have developed this to a fine art now, and it is fascinating to figure out how a particular mail shot has been generated. Often information from several different files must be used automatically by the computer to bring together in a single letter the main text, your name and address from a mailing list file, and perhaps the name and address of your nearest dealer from a dealer file.

Next time you get a mail shot from *Time-Life, Readers Digest* or a car maker, see if you can spot the joins between standard text and text tailored to your address. Direct mail is a specialized business relying more on automatic data processing than on conventional word processing. Word processing allows the operator to interact with the text on screen, but this too requires several files of information to be available. Stuck for the right word to use? Type the nearest you can think of straight off, then invoke the thesaurus. Your PC will refer to the thesaurus file and display a dozen or more nearly equivalent words. Point to the word you want and the PC can automatically insert it in place of the word you first thought of. It can also find and replace, if necessary, all other occurrences of a particular word, wherever it occurs in a document.

Uncertain about the spelling of a word? Invoke the spell checker and your PC will refer to its dictionary file to check that a particular word, or every word, in your document is a real word. It will spot 'beleive' and ask if you want to replace it with 'believe', but will pass over 'rain' even when you should have used 'reign'. PCs are not very good at interpreting context yet, but they are getting better. Programs are available which will check your writing style; these mostly do simple things like checking average word, sentence and paragraph length, but they can also spot split infinitives and long dependent clauses.

It is the simple things word processors do well, like finding and replacing a particular word, name, or string of characters. For instance, in a long report appraising a computer project, you might wish to remove a jargon term and replace it with something more generally understandable. 'Find and replace' allows you to key in the string to be found, and also the string to replace it with. The computer can then find every occurrence of the jargon term, 'DCF return', say, and replace it with 'internal rate of return'. For a 10,000 word report which would take you an hour or more just to read, finding and replacing can be completed by your word processor in seconds.

Saving

If we wish to describe word processing in 'systems' terminology, then text entry at the keyboard is the input, editing is the process, and printing is the output. It is the input stage, involving manual text entry which is the bottleneck; and that is why cheap storage on disk has been developed. Once the text has been entered, it can be processed, stored, accessed and printed with great ease and at lightning speed.

So, as a general rule, you should never just print a hard copy of a word processing session. Always save any work at the keyboard – either after entering original text, or after an editing session. Then you can avoid ever having to type out in full the same or similar text again. For all but the smallest of files it is easier and much cheaper to edit an old file stored on disk than it is to type it out again. The only exceptions are very short two- or three-line memos and the like, which may be cheaper to re-type than to access from disk – especially if the disk space is cluttered up with thousands of other two or three liners.

When you save a file you have to think of a unique name for it, a name which will be easy for you to locate again when you need it. We will return to the topic of file names when we discuss file organization later, but it is worth mentioning at this point that if you try to save a new file with the same name as an old file, the new file will replace, or overwrite, the old file. This situation commonly arises when you need to produce a letter, say, which is similar but not the same as an existing one. To save a lot of repetitive typing, you could pull out the original letter, edit and print it, then save it. But the new version displayed on-screen would overwrite and lose the original version held on disk, unless you save the new version under a different name.

In this brief introduction to word processing we have seen how information in the form of text is accessed, edited and saved. Other forms of information such as numbers or graphics are processed in almost exactly the same way. Let us start with numbers.

Spreadsheets

The most popular software for handling numbers and graphs on PCs is the spreadsheet, which manipulates numbers and formulae in all the same ways that a word processor manipulates text. For instance, you can insert and delete, copy or move blocks of numbers and so on, which is great for dealing with tables of figures. But if that was all a spreadsheet could do, you could manage almost as easily with your word processor.

The big extra advantage that spreadsheets offer is their ability to interpret numbers as values which, unlike words, can be added, subtracted, displayed as a graph, sorted into order of value, averaged, etc. – that is, used in calculations to derive useful results for decision-making and control.

Entering data

When you switch on and first load the spreadsheet software package, you are presented with an empty screen – as happens with many word processors – only this time the screen is divided up into columns and rows – in some ways a bit like the squared paper we first used for arithmetic at primary school. Each column has an identifying letter A, B, C, etc., at the top, and each row is numbered, so that each square or 'cell' has its own address. For instance, the first or 'home' cell at the top left of the screen where column A crosses row 1 has the address A1.

There are three different types of entry you can make in a cell:

- A label – alphanumeric characters, usually a name or column heading.
- A value – numbers, which can be used in calculations.

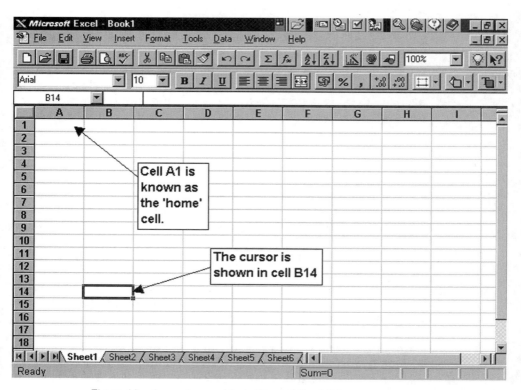

Figure 4.5   *An empty spreadsheet: Microsoft Excel 7.0*

● A formula – e.g. =A2 + A3. The result will be displayed, not the formula.

It is this ability to enter formulae using cell addresses as variables that makes spreadsheets so wonderfully versatile. For instance, the example above, =A2 + A3, entered in cell A1 would cause the sum of the values currently entered in cells A2 and A3 to be displayed in cell A1.

Also, as mentioned in Chapter 3, there is one other special type of formula you can use with spreadsheets, which will derive functions of values entered, such as:

● The average of a set of values.
● The standard deviation of a set of values.
● The logarithm of a value.

Modern spreadsheet packages hold a library of these special functions, making it possible for you to construct spreadsheet programs to perform quite sophisticated analyses of numerical data.

One example of analysis which is very commonly performed on a spreadsheet is cash-flow forecasting, which was featured right at the beginning of this book in the opening scenario with the executive performing 'what-if' analysis and worrying about costs and margins.

Cash is very important. Running out of cash can bring an organization to its knees quicker than becoming loss-making or unprofitable. Without cash an organization cannot pay its employees and will cease to operate. That is why cash-flow forecasting is so useful: it analyses future income and expenditure month by month to check that, on average, there is a positive flow of cash into the organization, and that cash balances will be adequate to cover any months when cash flow is expected to be negative.

Cash-flows are normally constructed for a year or more into the future, to calculate the effects of anticipated income and expenditure each month on the current account. We know we will receive bills in the future; we know their likely size and when they will arrive. We also know roughly how much revenue to expect from forecasted sales, and when it will be paid to us. So we allocate 12 columns of cells on the spreadsheet to the 12 months of the forecast period, one column for each month. Then in the first column for the first month, we make two lists, one for all the income we expect to receive, and another for all the expenses we must meet (Figure 4.6). By entering formulae at the foot of each list, we can get the spreadsheet to produce the totals of income and expense for the month.

We can also enter a formula to display the difference between income and expense, which is called the cash flow for the month. If income is greater than expense, the cash flow in that month is positive, and if smaller it is negative. The cash flow can then be used to adjust the balance of the current account at the end of that month.

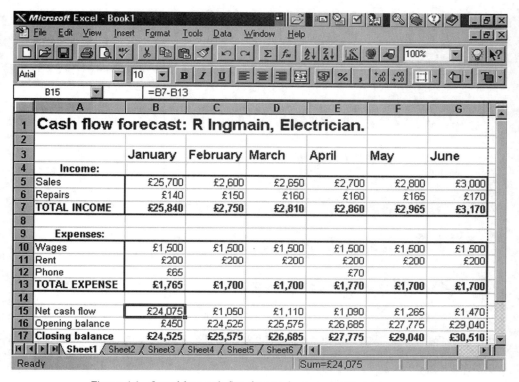

Figure 4.6 *Spreadsheet cash flow forecast for Ingmain, Electrician*

So, our spreadsheet shows for January the total income, total expenditure, cash flow and the balance of the current account at the beginning and end of the month. The balance at the end of January – called the closing balance for January – will of course be the opening balance for February. You can get the spreadsheet to carry the value forward by simply typing the address of the cell where it appeared before into the cell where you want it to appear again. For instance in Figure 4.7, you can see that in cell C16, the formula =B17 has been entered. This carries forward the closing balance in January calculated in cell B17, to use as the opening balance for February displayed in cell C16.

Once you have worked out the formulae you need and entered them into the January column of the spreadsheet, you can then copy them all across to the other 11 columns for a 12-month forecast. This can be done very easily.

To copy cells in Microsoft Excel, you first select the cells with the mouse. The selected cells appear with a black border round them. To copy the selected cells, you simply drag the border along the row, and the contents of the cells will be copied.

The cash flow forecast is a kind of financial model of your operations, and you can play with it assuming different favourable or

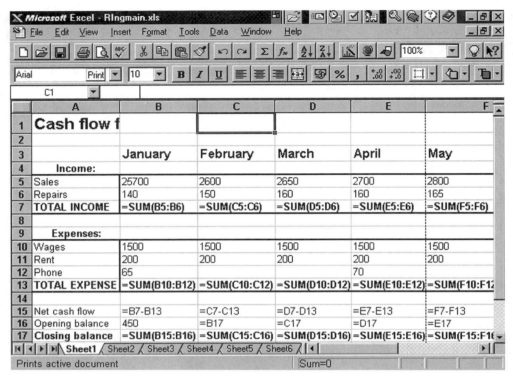

Figure 4.7   *Excel displays the formulae for the Ingmain forecast*

Cash flow forecast: R Ingmain, Electrician

Income:	January	February	March	April	May	June
Sales	£25,700	£2,600	£2,650	£2,700	£2,800	£3,000
Repairs	£140	£150	£160	£160	£165	£170
TOTAL INCOME	**£25,840**	**£2,750**	**£2,810**	**£2,860**	**£2,965**	**£3,170**
Expenses:						
Wages	£1,500	£1,500	£1,500	£1,500	£1,500	£1,500
Rent	£200	£200	£200	£200	£200	£200
Phone	£65			£70		
TOTAL EXPENSE	**£1,765**	**£1,700**	**£1,700**	**£1,770**	**£1,700**	**£1,700**
Net cash flow	£24,075	£1,050	£1,110	£1,090	£1,265	£1,470
Opening balance	£450	£24,525	£25,575	£26,685	£27,775	£29,040
CLOSING BALANCE	**£24,525**	**£25,575**	**£26,685**	**£27,775**	**£29,040**	**£30,510**

Figure 4.8   *The spreadsheet results as printed in a report*

unfavourable circumstances. For instance, what will happen if labour costs or interest rates go up? What effect will this have on your cash balance month by month? Will you have to negotiate an increase in your overdraft limit with the bank? When you play 'what-if' with your model in this way, you develop a feel for how sensitive your operations are to, for example, an increase in interest rates, and if necessary take action to reduce exposure to this risk. Also, once you have developed what you believe to be the most likely scenario, you can print out the spreadsheet results, perhaps for inclusion in a financial report (Figure 4.8).

Not long ago, cash-flow forecasts were drawn up using pencil and paper – an extremely tedious job involving much rubbing out and re-entering of values. What-if analysis just was not feasible; it would have taken far too long. Now though, multiple versions of the same analysis can be produced in minutes. Just by changing a figure here or there, the formulae in the spreadsheet will re-calculate the whole analysis on the basis of the new figures, and the effect on the current account on the bottom line is displayed immediately.

Accessing, editing and saving

When you have developed your spreadsheet you will want to save it on disk. Otherwise it will be lost when you switch off or close the application and change to word processing for instance, or even clear the screen to work on another spreadsheet problem. Remember, when you are interacting with data on the screen, those data only exist in the live memory circuits – the RAM of the computer – so if you want to keep your work, you must save it to disk.

Even if you don't anticipate needing the work again, you should save your work as a matter of course. It is so easy to do: all you need to do with Microsoft programs is to click with the mouse pointer on the little diskette icon near the top left of the screen. Then if you have not already provided a name for the file to be saved under, a dialogue box will prompt you to do so. The file name you provide will allow you to call it back again if you need it. It is much easier to find your work again if you give meaningful names to your files.

Don't forget you have to be careful when saving an edited version of an old file, or you can lose the old version by overwriting it with the new version. If you want to keep the old and the new versions, don't just click on the diskette icon, or use the 'Save' command. Use the 'Save as . . .' command instead. This ensures the dialogue box opens and you get a chance to change the file name before the file is saved to disk.

Recalling a file is easy. Just click on the 'File' pull-down menu at the top of the screen. If you have been using the file recently, its name will appear on the menu and all you need do is click on it. If it is a file you have not been using recently, its name will not appear in the menu, and you will need to click on 'Open...' in the menu instead.

This will bring up a dialogue box which allows you to tell the computer where to look for your file – which disk drive and which directory for instance.

The file name you gave your file will appear with a full stop at the end followed by a three-letter extension. Microsoft Excel adds .xls (standing for Excel spreadsheet presumably), so for instance if you chose to call your file CASHFLOW the file would actually appear on the disk directory as CASHFLOW.XLS

Graphs

The values produced by your spreadsheet can be displayed in a variety of ways as pie, bar, line and scatter diagrams for instance.

It is possible to save several graphs as different ways of presenting information from the same spreadsheet. These graphs are saved in the same file as, and are linked to, the spreadsheet itself. Thus if you change a value in the spreadsheet, a previously prepared graph will adjust in shape to reflect the change.

Other software packages

There are many other types of software that you can buy to run on your PC which will allow you to use it for a great variety of different tasks. We cannot cover them all, so let us just take a quick look at a few of the more common applications:

● Databases.
● Accounting systems.
● Project management software.
● Computer-aided design (CAD).
● Desktop publishing.
● Multimedia.
● The Internet.

Databases

The easiest way of understanding a database is to think of it performing rather like a kind of electronic card index system (Figure 4.9). Indeed there is a database package called Cardbox, but probably the better known ones are such products as Access, Oracle and Dataease. A computer database is far superior to the card box though. Not only does it automate the search procedure and do it in a tiny fraction of the time it would take to do manually, but it can also perform searches which would be almost impossible to do manually.

Here's a case in point. Long before computers were around, small businesses such as a local garage used to keep records in a card index.

**Computer records are held in a 'database'
– a kind of electronic card index**

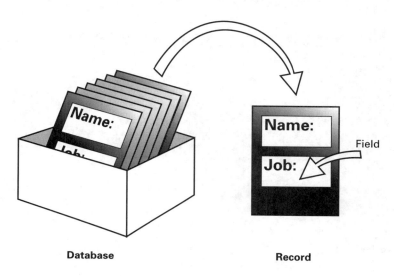

Database

Record

Figure 4.9   *Databases, records and fields*

There would be a card for each customer, showing the customer's full name and address. The card might also hold other information such as the registration number of the cars owned by each customer, and perhaps a record of work done and invoices paid. The cards would be filed in alphabetical order of surname, so that a customer's records could be accessed quickly should the customer phone or call in.

But supposing a new mechanic needs to find out which customer owns a particular car on the forecourt which has the registration number P 123 ABC for instance. The card index is very little help, because although all the registration numbers are held on the cards, the cards are in alphabetical order of surname, and that is what the mechanic is trying to find out! He could start searching through the index from the beginning, As first, then Bs and so on until he found it, but that would take forever. With a computer database however, you could key in either the customer's surname or the car registration number. The customer's record would appear just as quickly either way.

This is the strength of the database. It holds information in such a way that you can search through it in all sorts of imaginative ways which would not be feasible with a card index system. Let's take a quick look at two examples of how databases are routinely used by many organizations – in sales and in human resources.

Sales representatives must keep records of the names of their clients, along with other details such as personal preferences, future plans

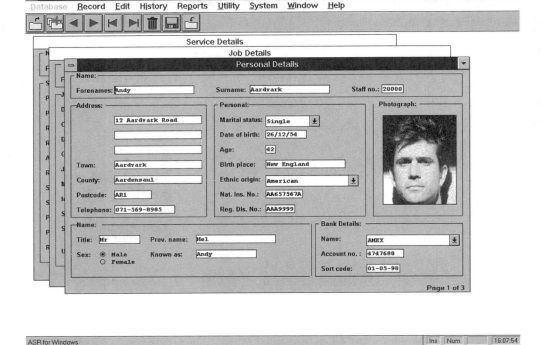

Figure 4.10   *Example of a database. The ASR personnel information system*

and past transactions. The records might show the name and address of the contact, the products bought, the date of the last visit and the value of orders placed during the last year.

Now suppose a representative has an appointment in Hatfield and, to make best use of the journey, wants to make other visits in the same area. With a database it would be possible to list all customers in Hertfordshire. Or, if there were too many, the computer could be asked to display all customers in Hertfordshire who had not been visited in the last three months. Or perhaps better still, all customers in Hertfordshire who had placed orders of greater than £10,000 in the last year, but who had not bought product X and had not been visited in the last month. This is support of real value, with great potential to improve the efficiency and productivity of the sales team.

Similar benefits are being realized in human resources (HR) and personnel departments. The old ring binders and filing cabinets full of staff records have mostly gone now, and have been replaced by a database (Figure 4.10). For security this is often located on a stand-alone PC in the HR department, but it is also possible to put the database on an organization-wide information system, with sensitive information protected of course by access codes available only to authorized staff.

This is another example of how storing information digitally opens up new ways of working. Because it is easy to restrict access to medical histories and salaries, it becomes possible to give wide access to data on skills and competencies. Thus a line manager looking for someone to replace a leaver, or someone who is fluent in French, can query the database directly, instead of having to wait for the HR department to supply the information. This accessibility of information is very attractive to progressive organizations experimenting with non-hierarchical structures of multi-skilled teams. It speeds up decision-making throughout the organization, and is the driving force behind business process re-engineering.

Personnel administration yields to self-service HR

Personnel departments used to be quiet staff backwaters, cut off from the turbulent mainstream of operations. But once the dusty personnel folders went digital, the floodgates were opened, and the job could never be the same again.

Of course they anticipated that putting employee information on the PC would improve speed and efficiency by automating some tasks, but they didn't foresee individual employees filling in and maintaining their own records, or line managers searching the files for themselves. But this is exactly what they do at PWA Personnel Systems – and of course they will be delighted to sell you a system to do the same in your organization.

But why should you want to? Because you want to survive in today's fast-moving business environment, perhaps? Devolved responsibility means people really are your most valuable resource, and to do their job they need information.

Line managers need to know what the attrition rate is in their departments, and whether they are losing the poor performers or the high-flyers. Decision-makers need the information now, not next week. By the time a written report comes through, decisions have already been made.

Employees are better, faster and cheaper at maintaining their personal records. It's in their interests to keep their experience, skills and training records accurate and up-to-date. And of course it benefits the organization when it is sure of what competences it has available.

The old bureaucracies governed by secrecy and fear are being replaced by multi-skilled teams, empowered by easy access to information in a more open and trusting regime, even in big companies. National Semiconductor is going global with its new personal access HR software from SAP, and so is IBM with HR Access software from CGI, a company they own. All employees will eventually be responsible for maintaining their basic details, with line managers also entering salary changes and performance reviews for their staff.

It's just good business and sensible use of technology.

These then are examples of queries that any database is designed to handle. Of course a card index or a filing system could hold just the same data, but they would be inaccessible, and therefore useless for the new ways of working which, because of their enormous potential, are prevailing over the old methods.

Accounting systems

Nearly every business, large or small, has one of these nowadays. Big organizations have big systems on the mainframe run by the finance department, while small businesses run a package such as Sage or Pegasus on their PC.

These packages make it possible to maintain up-to-date records of purchases, sales, stock levels, payrolls and time keeping. The system will require purchase orders, invoices and wage slips to be produced using the system, and in this way the ledgers are all kept up to date automatically by the computer.

Apart from solving many of the filing problems associated with running a business, these packages also save money by automating the production of routine reports, such as quarterly VAT tax returns, and the usual end of year profit and loss accounts, and balance sheets.

These systems also produce management reports, such as lists of stock items which are getting low, and lists of overdue debtors. This support for routine decision-making is essential to the efficiency of any organization.

Project management

If you are ever put in charge of a 'project' and you can work with a PC, get some project management software. It will pay for itself many times over.

So what kind of work qualifies as project? Here are a few examples:

● Launching a new product or service.
● Overhauling operational equipment.
● Constructing a new building.

- Re-locating an office.
- Installing a computer system.
- Conducting a training programme.

Thus any new work is a project if it lasts for a limited period, involves different groups of workers, and has penalties for late completion. The project manager is responsible for first planning, then controlling the allocation of time, money, people and other resources.

Managing a project is difficult because with new work there are few clear precedents to follow. Also, the people working on the project are often seconded part time and thus have other responsibilities and other bosses to please, in addition to their project responsibilities. So, all in all, as a project manager you will need all the help you can get.

There are dozens of packages available. Some of the better known ones are Microsoft Project, SuperProject Expert from Computer Associates, MacProject for the Apple Macintosh, and Artemis from Metier. They all require the project to be defined in terms of a list of the component activities that must be carried out, together with activity durations and dependency links.

The software then constructs a critical path network (see Chapter 2) and uses it as the basis for providing decision support for the project manager.

For instance, you can have a printout of the activities displayed as bars arranged on a Gantt chart, as shown earlier in Figure 2.11. Also, you can enter details of the resources allocated to each activity – the number of hours of each named person's time for instance – and get back a report of exactly when each resource is required.

Most packages can handle several projects all at the same time, and will warn if conflicting demands are made for the same resource. Where conflicts do arise, the software makes it simple to make adjustments, or to re-plan the project according to new priorities. This is really useful support – information processing at its most meaningful from a management point of view.

Computer aided design

Want to plan a new office layout? Or sketch an idea for a design? Then you will need a drawing board, a ruler for measuring, compasses, pencils, erasers, etc. Or you could use a computer aided design (CAD) package to develop your design on the screen of your PC before printing it.

CAD packages use just the same processes as your word processor or spreadsheet. Your work will be saved in files and, if you want to produce a design which is similar to something you have done before, you can save time by editing an old file.

Also, you can mark a section of a drawing to repeat it or move it or delete it in much the same way as your word processor allows you electronically to cut and paste blocks of text. The only difference is that CAD packages are designed for manipulating graphics entities – arcs, lines, circles, etc. – rather than text or numbers.

CAD packages can be awkward to use if the only input device you have is a keyboard. The keyboard was designed for inputting text and numerals, not graphics entities. For these you really need a mouse – a hand-held device you can move around on top of your desk. Then, selecting a graphics entity is easy: you just point and click. Move the mouse, and a pointer on the screen moves with it. You select from a palette of graphics options displayed on the screen by pointing and clicking with the mouse. Alternatively, the mouse itself may be fitted with cross-hair sights which you aim over the desired palette option mounted on a special tablet.

If you are thinking of buying a graphics package, there are a number of different types available, some of which make freehand sketching easy, and some which are more suitable for producing line drawings to scale for engineers and architects. Autocad is a well-known package for engineers and architects; Harvard Graphics is very popular in business for reports and presentations; and software with the words 'draw' or 'paint' in the title are usually more suitable for freehand work.

Desktop publishing

This is the software for you if you want to combine text and pictures to produce a newsletter or house magazine, or high-quality reports and sales literature. In the past, the only way was to write the text yourself and then get a typesetter and printer to design the page layout for you and print in the quantities you required. Now, with the right software and a suitable laser printer you can do it all yourself. However, page layout is an art and you need an eye for design to produce really professional results.

Not long ago there was a big difference between word processors and desktop publishers. Now the gap has narrowed. Most modern word processors have some graphics capabilities and can set text in multiple columns in different fonts and typeface styles. Desktop publishing though can still offer much better ability to handle line and half-tone pictures. To get the half-tones into digital form you may need a scanner. Once you have the pictures on disk you can manipulate them just the same as other features to appear on the page: you can enlarge, contract, rotate, reproduce, relocate and so on.

Communications software

Poor communications – people not telling other people what they're up to – has long been a problem within organizations. People feel left out when they have the results of decisions thrust upon them out of the blue, and the result is damaged morale and motivation. In the hierarchical days of the industrial era, managers could get away with issuing cryptic commands, but it won't do now in this new age of information and teamwork. Teams cannot compete without copious, free, high-quality communications. Fortunately, the engine of the information era – the computer – has a big role to play here.

In the early 1980s, many organizations had only a big mainframe computer, used mostly to automate clerical work of various types. Different departments such as accounts, sales and production were given access to the mainframe via remote terminals. The terminal was just a screen and keyboard in the department on the end of a long cable from the computer, and often managers found themselves competing amongst themselves for data processing services. So when the PC became available, managers saw it as a stand-alone solution that was cheap enough to buy from their own budget, allowing them to solve their own problems and avoid the need to go cap in hand to the high priests of the corporate mainframe.

PCs appeared overnight like mushrooms throughout the organization, and mainframe terminals were used less and less. Worried mainframe staff looked for a role in the new world of personal computing – and they found it in the need to wire up several PCs to a single printer, as at that time printers were expensive and under-utilized when only connected to one PC. These local area networks (LANs) also allowed files to be transferred from one computer to another. However in these early days, setting up communications links between computers was a complex and arcane business which made the user dependent on specialist computer staff again, and few users then would choose to be linked to a network if they could have their own printer. In practice, even when connected, users often preferred to exchange files on diskettes rather than tangle with the network.

Today, however, the technicalities are much easier. Communications protocols are standardized, and with the right software and cables users can plug into the network for themselves. And that is what they want to do, because now the benefits far outweigh the costs. Easier, freer communications bring efficiencies for the individual as well as the organization by saving on editing, printing and photocopying memos and reports. But also, faster, more timely communications make teams much more effective, which is essential in today's fast-moving business environment.

Price Waterhouse foresaw future network needs

Price Waterhouse (PW) is one of the 'big six' consultancy firms in the world, serving many multinational clients around the globe.

PW employs 7000 people in the UK and 46,000 world-wide, people whose job it is to provide clients with cost-effective business solutions.

Thus, in 1987 when planning to replace 1000 word processors throughout the UK, PW was able to avoid an ineffective solution to managing their own business. They realized they could do better than simply buy 1000 new PCs.

'The core part of our business is sharing information between ourselves and the client,' asserts Steve Davies, senior manager of the Management Services Division. 'The industry was at that time only just getting into standalone PCs. Contention between standalone PCs and networking was quite apparent – standalone PCs would improve facilities but limit flexibility', says Davies. 'People were already saying that perhaps in a few years time they were going to need to share data and resources and shift documents back and forth. We had no doubt that we would have to do that at some point.'

'It appeared to be short-sighted to buy 1000 standalone PCs (which at that time were about £2000 apiece) and spend money linking them up with printers, when in three years we knew we would be spending yet more money on establishing a network. What we really wanted to do was network them today for no extra money.' The sums added up, and PW was able to install networked word processing under the Novell NetWare operating system.

Actual benefits at that time were a bit more difficult to demonstrate, admits Davies. 'It was very much printer sharing and that was it.' But five years down the line things have changed dramatically. Electronic mail is in use throughout the organization, and Lotus Notes allows groups of employees to share their work and create documents collectively. And with managers able to access information directly, they can respond efficiently and promptly to customer enquiries.

There are three main forms of internal communication enabled by the computer: the Intranet, based on technology developed for the Internet which we discussed earlier in this chapter; groupware, the software for group communications discussed in Chapter 2; and electronic mail, or e-mail as it is known, to distinguish it from the traditional paper-based 'snail-mail'.

The Internet is a global network, the best-known part of which is called the World Wide Web. The Web supports hypertext and multimedia communications, and has attracted huge public interest. It has stimulated development of Web 'browsers' which make it easy to search for and access files anywhere on the Web. New, easier, more efficient web browsers regularly appear, and the competition is fierce between software writers to produce the latest, most popular browser. As a result, Web browsers are so attractive and easy to use that organizations are now publishing 'Intranet' pages, similar to Internet pages, but only accessible to employees within the organization. Employees can then use their browsers to keep up to date with corporate news. Compared to a house magazine, this can be cheap, immediate, and more effective with sound and moving video. It can also allow instant feedback from user interaction.

The Intranet provides the means to address the whole organization team, but an organization of any size will operate as a team of smaller teams responsible for particular business processes. These smaller teams may consist of only six to twelve people perhaps, and have specific business communications needs which require particular computer solutions. For instance, automating the flow of work between members could bring benefits, or perhaps members may all need on-screen access to a design, a report or a software program as it is developed by the team. Or maybe desktop video computer conferencing would help a geographically distributed team to function more effectively. All these are examples of computer support for co-operative work (CSCW), or groupware. There are several suppliers of groupware products, of which perhaps Lotus Notes is the best known. However, some of the special features available in groupware packages, such as e-mail for instance, are now appearing in the system software supplied with PCs.

E-mail allows a PC user to type a message on screen and then send it through the network to arrive instantly with another user, or a mailing list of users. It is a new, additional form of communication which won't replace existing forms such as the phone or memo. However, it does have a particular mix of characteristics which can make it the most appropriate channel to use sometimes. It is more formal than a phone message, but less so than a memo. It avoids time wasted by playing telephone tag, but cannot convey the subtle nuances and intonations of the spoken word. E-mail lacks the immediacy and intimacy of a phone conversation, and is more like a fax message than a phone call. And of course, nothing can ever replace the need for face-to-face meetings. Human closeness and the contact of a handshake will always be important in building the trust needed for people to co-operate and do business together.

File organization

In this chapter we have mentioned files many times. As you know, all software and data and any work saved on disk is held in files. It is worth saying a few words about how these should be arranged so that you can find them again easily when necessary.

File names

Microsoft Windows 95 allows file names of up to 255 characters, including spaces. This is a welcome improvement on the eight plus three characters allowed by the old Windows 3.11 user interface and its underlying DOS operating system. However, even if you are using Windows 95 the people you wish to exchange files with may not have it, and so for a while it will still be important for you to understand the limitations of DOS.

DOS restricts file names to a maximum of eight alphanumeric characters, plus an optional three character extension. For instance FILENAME.EXT is valid, and shorter names such as FILE are also valid. Here are some other filenames which are valid under DOS:

FRED.004
F.4
F2
F.2A8
ACCOUNTS.XLS

DOS will not allow spaces or full-stops in a filename, except for the full-stop just before the extension. So, for example, the following file names would be invalid:

DAN.DARE
DARE DAN
KEEP OUT

With Windows 95, however, you are free to choose almost any file name you wish, up to 255 characters long. A file name this long would cover about three lines on your screen! Also, another new feature is that you can use upper and lower case characters, whereas DOS made no distinction between them. Now, for instance, you can use file names like these if you wish:

My letter to Aunt. Mary, thanking her for my Xmas present.
1997 Cashflow. Sales Dept

There are still ten characters which Windows 95 will not allow you to use in file names. They are the forward slash (/), back slash (\), greater than (>), less than (<), asterisk (*), question mark (?), quotation mark ('), pipeline symbol (¦), colon (:), and semi-colon (;). Also, if there is any chance your file will be used by someone without Windows 95, they will see your long file names cut back to the old eight plus three limit, with the shortened version showing only the first six characters from your long file name (not counting spaces). Thus the above two examples of long file names would appear as:

MYLETT~1.DOC
1997CA~1.XLS

or something similar. So when exchanging files, make the first six characters significant.

If you have ever used Word or Excel you will know these programs automatically attach a three-character extension to your file names. For instance, Word adds .doc and Excel adds .xls as extensions. Applications programs use the extensions to avoid opening or listing the wrong type of file, so you should avoid adding or changing a file name extension with File Manager or Explorer, unless you know what the effects will be. For instance, some extensions are reserved for system files. The ones to avoid are:

.COM
.EXE
.BAT
.SYS

For instance, a document named CRICKET.BAT might cause problems.

Here are some other common conventions for the use of the extension:

● Word processors often keep two copies of your files: one from the last time you saved your work, and the one from the time before last. This earlier copy is given the same filename as the file you are working on but is given the extension .BAK to indicate that it is a back-up copy in case you lose the latest version.
● README.TXT indicates that the file README is a text file that can be read directly just by double-clicking on its listing in File Manager or Explorer.
● CASHFLOW.BAS indicates that the file is a program written in the BASIC programming language.
● TEST.DAT indicates that the file contains data.
● FLOWER.BMP is a bit-map graphics file, in this case a picture of a flower.

With experience you will learn to recognize many other file extensions.

Folders

You may have hundreds of files on a single floppy diskette, but possibly thousands on your hard disk. In order to find them easily when you need them, it makes sense to group files together in different categories. For instance, you might put all word-processed documents together in one group, and spreadsheet files in another group. Then, you might like to go a step further and divide up your word-processed documents into groups, a separate group for each customer or client perhaps, just as you might file letters and reports in customer folders in a conventional filing cabinet.

With DOS and Windows 3.11 these groupings of files were called Directories, but in Windows 95 they are called Folders. This is because unlike the old Directory system, which worked more like a telephone directory, Folders are true objects which can be cut, copied, moved and pasted, just like any other object. This makes it much easier to share work on the network, move an entire project to a new location, or make copies for your colleagues. However, until you learn how to use these extra facilities, there is no harm in using Folders just as you used to use Directories.

In this chapter we have dealt mostly with the PC, and only made occasional reference to networks and mainframes. However, your PC at work is probably only part of a system of computers which has an architecture designed to function as a management information system for the whole organization. In the next chapter we will consider what you as a manager need to know about this overall system and its architecture.

Competence self-assessment

1 What is the main application that managers use PCs for? Why is this inappropriate?

2 Write a line or two to describe in general how computers support decision-making by helping managers to:

● Find information.
● Analyse information.
● Store information.

3 If there are PCs where you work, find out the following about them:

● Do they have Windows 95, or some other user interface?
● Are they networked?
● What software do they run? What is the name of the word processor, the spreadsheet, the database, and any other software?
● How much memory do the PCs have. That is, what size RAM in kilobytes or megabytes?
● What are they mostly used for?

4

Sit down at the keyboard of a PC, and see if you can carry out the following routine word-processing functions. You will have to refer to the user guide to find the right commands for the particular word processor you are using. If possible, have someone around who can help if you get into difficulty.

(a) Switch on and start up the word processor.
(b) Type a few lines of text and save it under the file name MYFIRST.
(c) Close the file on screen, so your screen is clear.
(d) Retrieve the file MYFIRST from disk. When you do this, the original stays on the disk and a duplicate is created in RAM which you see on the screen so you can edit and modify it.
(e) Move the cursor through the text of your file. Find out how to move around quickly and precisely inside your document. Practise using the mouse to perform the following operations:

- Move the display up and down a line at a time, and a screen at a time.
- Select a phrase, then drag and drop it at a new position in the text.
- Select a word and use the thesaurus to replace it with an alternative word.
- Put a wrongly spelt word in the text, then use the system to correct it automatically.
- Select all the text and change the font style and point size.
- Move the margins and justify the text to display it as a narrow column.
- Select and delete a phrase – then undo the delete automatically to restore the phrase.

(f) Save this edited file under the new file name MYSECOND. Check the files on disk. Your original MYFIRST and the edited version MYSECOND should both be there. Now delete them both.

5

Sit down at a PC equipped with spreadsheet software. Again you should have an experienced user around to help if at all possible.

(a) Switch on and start up the spreadsheet.
(b) In cell A1 type in a value, say 150. In cell A2 type in another value, say 25. In cell A3 type in =A1+A2. You should see the value 175 appear.
(c) In cell A4 type in your name.
(d) Use the mouse to select cell A1. Then drag and drop the contents into cell D5.
(e) Now give your spreadsheet file a name and save it. Clear your screen and check you can retrieve your saved file again.
(f) Quit and switch off.

References and further reading

Beekman, G. (1994). *Computer Currents. Navigating Tomorrow's Technology.* Benjamin/ Cummings.

Norton, P. (1995). *Peter Norton's complete guide to Windows 95.* Sams.

Beekman gives a comprehensive description of the many ways in which computers are used today. Any lay person should feel comfortable with this friendly book. Nearly every page has colour pictures, charts and photographs which really bring the text to life.

Norton's guide is a knowledgeable text, but not for the technologically faint-hearted. Those new to computers should stick to the 'Help' option available when you start up Windows 95.

5 Moulding the system to your needs

Why is this chapter relevant?

British managers are not famous for their long-term business planning and decision-making. The press often comments that poor economic performance in the UK is in part due to short-termism. This may be true, but it is not clear what you or I should do about it: often we are forced into that mode by short-term financial targets imposed upon us.

However, when it comes to management information systems (MIS) we really must plan ahead. To provide satisfactory customer service increasingly depends on making appropriate use of up-to-date technology, and the technology is developing at break-neck speed. It is verging on suicidal not to look ahead.

It is easy to overlook the staggering rate at which computers are developing – and costs continue to tumble. In the 1950s, a Univac computer cost $2.5 million. By 1980 you could buy the same performance on a single circuit board costing $500. By comparison, a Rolls-Royce costing $28,000 in 1950 should now cost $5 and run for three million miles on a single gallon of fuel.

The useful life of your information system at work – that network of computers which forms the nervous system of your organization – will last only for a few years. During the next five years or so, you will almost certainly be involved in the development or replacement of your system. This chapter will help you acquire a broader perspective, sounder judgement and greater confidence when making your contribution to new systems development.

The life cycle of an information system

Information systems should not be allowed to just grow as a natural outcome of conducting business. Such an approach always results in a complete mess of incompatible subsystems, with some functions duplicated and others missed out altogether. The only reliable way is to have the system designed and installed by a team of specialists who know about business and also about computers.

There are three main stages in an information systems project:

● First, analysing how the whole business is run.
● Then designing on paper a suitable computer system.
● Then, buying the hardware, installing and commissioning it.

To these three stages, we can add two more: a preliminary feasibility study before committing to the expense of a full-blown analysis of the business; and a final maintenance stage to keep the system running satisfactorily after it has been installed. The complete systems life cycle therefore consists of five stages:

1 Feasibility study.
2 Business analysis.
3 Systems design.
4 Implementation.
5 Maintenance.

The project team

If you work in an organization big enough to have its own computing department, you may be able to put together a project team entirely from your own staff. Smaller organizations, however, must get help from outside, preferably from reputable independent consultants. It is nice to be able to choose, but both approaches have their advantages.

Putting together your own project team is normally cheaper. Also, you keep the specialist knowledge in your organization and this can be useful in the later maintenance phase after the consultants have left. However, if you bring in consultants, you can benefit from their breadth of experience of analysing, designing and implementing systems in many other organizations. Thus your project will benefit from, and add to, their experience as they pry into every corner of your business during the analysis phase. Of course their professional reputation is at stake so their confidentiality should be beyond question. The benefits of employing reputable consultants are that they can provide structure and methodology to the project. Also they represent additional human resources which are valuable to cover the extra work outside the normal run of your business generated by the project during its intensive middle stages.

Even if you do employ consultants, you cannot hand the whole job to them: your staff must be well represented on the project team. The team will be led by a project manager, and should consist of:

● System users.
● Business analysts.
● Systems designers.
● Computer programmers and engineers.

Users are at the top of the list. They must get a system at the end in which they've had a big say in designing, and they feel they 'own'. Sometimes a misguided steering committee will try to impose a system without consulting the users sufficiently. This approach is highly likely to fail; the best system in the world will fail if the users feel it is being used to spy on them or control them. They will use their ingenuity to find ways of defeating the system or circumventing it.

Another danger is that the computer professionals can get the bit between their teeth and charge off towards some technologically sophisticated dream solution. This too is likely to result in unsatisfactory performance. The users must believe in the benefits of the system and see it as a useful tool to help them do a better job.

It is the performance of the total human–computer system that matters, not just the computers. For the best chance of success the project team must gain total commitment and wholehearted co-operation from the users. Then the users will apply their ingenuity to make the system work, even if it turns out to be less than ideal from a purely technological point of view.

There is only one way of gaining the full support of users: they must be continually involved from the earliest stages of the project, with real influence in its design, all the way through to the end. This inevitably means the project will take longer to complete, but like the ha'pennyworth of tar to stop the ship sinking, it really is essential.

Organizing the project

The project manager will report directly to a steering committee consisting of senior executives (Figure 5.1).

The direct costs of a major systems project will always be large, often a significant percentage of annual turnover. Also, the system may be essential for basic functions like invoicing and budgeting – activities to do with cash flow, the life blood of the organization. There are very real risks if the system does not function satisfactorily, and

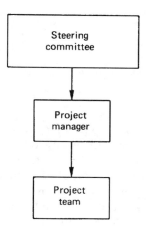

Figure 5.1   *Project organization chart*

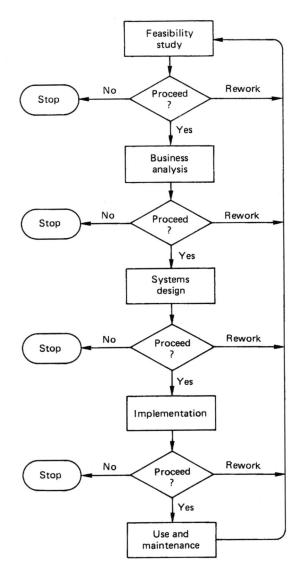

Figure 5.2   *Steering committee control of a project*

so the steering committee must have the power of veto, to halt the project at the end of any one of the five stages of the project. The project team must therefore prepare a report for the steering committee at the end of each stage, with two or three suggestions for the next stage, one of which should be recommended for approval by the steering committee (Figure 5.2).

We will return to examine how the project is controlled through the five stages of the life cycle, but first let us review how computers initially came to be used in business. Technology is still developing very rapidly and has a big influence on the design of information systems, so to get a feel for where business computing is headed, you should know where it came from.

The birth and upbringing of the business computer

Conception

In 1958 there were just 160 computers in the whole of Europe, and only the very biggest companies could even think about using them – mostly for scientific applications. All organizations used paper-work systems for recording and distributing the information they needed. These systems were operated by an army of clerks, secretaries, mail boys and teams of girls in finance with the strange title of 'comptometer operator', who spent the day tapping away on adding machines. Information was stored in filing cabinets and plan chests, was accessed by asking a secretary to pull out the needed files or drawings, and was communicated through circulation lists and the internal mail system.

Embryo

By the late 1950s some businesses were waking up to the potential of these computers operated by scientists. Computers at that time were huge, unreliable monsters consuming so much power that the lights dimmed when they were switched on. They relied on thousands of radio valves that popped and fused like light bulbs. The machines seldom ran for more than a few hours between failures, and needed special premises and a large team of engineers to keep them going.

However, some businesses discovered that they could save on labour costs by buying time on these machines. They got access at economic rates to the number-crunching power of the scientists' computers, which proved ideal for routine accounting functions. The first business uses they were put to were the processing of payrolls and accounts receivable. Big savings were made in labour by automating clerical tasks, and one of the first jobs to disappear was that of the comptometer operator.

Birth

During the 1960s, organizations began to realize that computers could be applied to other routine tasks such as stock control and produc-tion control. Transistors replaced radio valves, making computers cheaper and more reliable, and so bigger companies began to set up their own data processing departments and operate their own computers. Thus the central mainframe was borne, operated by data processing staff offering a computing service to other department managers.

Infancy

By the late 1970s, more and more business tasks were being computerized. The transistor which had replaced the radio valve was itself being replaced, first by the integrated circuit and then by the microprocessor. These developments cut the costs of computing dramatically, while at the same time increasing their power and reliability.

Also, many department managers were beginning to get fed up of going cap in hand to the data processing citadel to beg small computing favours. They were beginning to find that computers were simple enough to run and had fallen in price sufficiently for them to buy and operate in their own departments, which freed them from being dependent on the data processing department. Separate computers were soon arriving in the design offices, the planning department, the sales office and so on.

This piecemeal approach to corporate computing came about because managers could make immediate savings in direct labour, at the same time as freeing themselves from dependence on the data processing department. Naturally, the data processing departments did what they could to resist this trend, because they could see their influence waning. But it was too late. The arrival of the PC in the early 1980s reduced even further the significance of the big central mainframe. The low cost and versatility of the PC meant they were popping up like mushrooms, everywhere. Soon computers were to be found in nearly every organization.

However, this could hardly be called a corporate approach to computing. The PCs were being used to automate the old paperwork systems, faults and all, and were reinforcing departmental boundaries. Each computer held its own separate files. The same information was being held many times over in different computers, with some versions obviously being more up to date than others. And to transfer data from one department to another involved printing out hard copy in the sending department and then re-keying the printed data back into the computer at the receiving department.

Adolescence

Today these so-called 'islands of automation' – separate computers in different departments – are being linked together via communications networks to form management information systems. The intention is that these integrated systems of computers should transcend departmental boundaries and allow data to be held at different points in the network, and yet be available through the network to all authorized users who might need it.

There is a concept known as single data entry for multiple users. In theory, it means that each data element held by the total system should only be held once. In practice, it is interpreted to mean that there should be the least possible duplication in the storage of data. If data are only entered and held once, in a single common database, there can only be one version of the state of play, available to all who need it. This will eliminate the confusions that can arise when earlier versions of modified records or drawings are allowed to remain in circulation. A common violation of the single data entry principle has, until recently, been the holding of two separate databases of employees – one for payroll and one for the human resources function. However, this is now being put right in progressive organizations where networks have been developed sufficiently for multi-skilled teams to replace specialist departments.

If 'bottom-up' implementation by department managers acting independently has progressed too far, it may pre-empt any 'top-down' planning for a corporate approach to the information needs of the organization as a whole. The many different hardware types, operating systems and incompatible software bought by different managers will make it almost impossible to link them up.

Business computing has yet to mature. It is still going through a dynamic period of growth and development. It can only be said to have matured when a set of standards have been developed for all manufacturers and users (like for cars, for instance), and development has slowed down. There are some signs that standards are emerging, despite development still proceeding unabated. For instance, the Windows user interface is becoming a widely adopted standard. Also, the Internet communications protocols known as X400 and TCP/IP could well become *de facto* standards for business communications. When operating a computer becomes intuitive, and plug-and-play hardware is the norm, we can claim that the industry is beginning to mature.

Controlling a computer system project

Let us start with an overview of the size of team required and the costs involved at different stages of the project (see Figure 5.3).

The feasibility study

This is a first quick look at the suitability of current methods of handling information, to see if they need modifying or changing. It involves only a few business analysts and systems designers.

The level of expenditure is very low, consisting of little more than the cost of the time logged by these individuals. Clearly no programming skills are needed at this stage – in fact the project manager and team will not yet have been recruited. Even so, it is important that

Phase	Team size	Typical proportion of total project costs (%)
Feasibility study	1 or 2 analysts	<5
Business analysis	Project manager + 3 or 4 analysts	10–15
System design	Project manager + analysts + programmers + users	25–30
Implementation	Project manager + analysts + programmers + users	55–60

Figure 5.3   *Team size and costs for each project phase*

the potential users of the new system are kept fully informed of the purpose of the study, and the opportunities for participation if the project goes ahead.

The feasibility study stage should close with a report to senior management, with a recommendation and alternative proposals, complete with an investment analysis consisting of an estimated internal rate of return and pay-back period.

A recommendation by senior management for the project to proceed will commit the organization to the costs of setting up the steering committee, appointing a project manger, and seconding members onto the project team. There will also be consultants' fees and other indirect costs.

The feasibility study should also provide senior management with a rough estimate of total project costs, which in principle they should be prepared to sanction if they recommend the project to proceed.

The business analysis

This will not involve any capital costs. The project is still at the investigation stage and can be thought of as a re-run in more detail of the feasibility study.

In fact this stage of the project will be concerned with three basic issues:

● Business objectives and philosophy.
● What is done now, and how it is done.
● What should be done, and how it could be done.

The type of skill required to investigate these issues is slightly different in each case. An experienced manager with business skills is required for the first phase, especially if there has been no corporate planning or formal statement of corporate objectives, as is often the case in young companies.

Does the organization set out to provide a high specification product at a high price, or a mid-range service competing on price? And how are these objectives to be achieved? By keeping tight control of bad debts? By monitoring closely the relationship between price and sales volume? Answers are needed to questions such as these, to use as system design criteria.

Floor staff at B&Q use hand-held computer terminals

Cordless system used to access stock details

B&Q is the UK's leading DIY retailer, a position they intend to keep by offering unrivalled service and total commitment to the customer. But in 1993, keeping track of stock was emerging as a problem. The company had 280 outlets, 16,000 employees, 12 million square feet of sales space – and plans for 75 giant 100,000 square foot warehouse stores, each carrying over 45,000 different stock items.

Stock control was managed entirely on a remote corporate IBM mainframe, with stock positions only updated at the end of each day. But to deliver unrivalled customer service, store staff needed more timely information than that, so B&Q invited tenders for a new system. After careful evaluation, they selected a powerful store-based system – the Oracle7 database on a Pentium PC server with about 20 client PCs.

The new system introduced in 1994, holds up-to-date details of a store's customer orders and inventory levels. Customer orders are flagged if there are changes to delivery dates or product availability, so the customer can be informed.

Inventory levels are right up to date. Items sold are deducted automatically via links with the store's electronic point of sale (EPOS) system. And deliveries coming in are added by floor staff using radio-frequency cordless hand-held terminals. Shop floor staff are pleased with the new system. Using the hand-held terminals to access current stock details, they can answer customer queries immediately.

And what of the corporate mainframe? It's still used, to exchange management and pricing data with each of the in-store databases during the night. Oracle forms the kernel of B&Q's future in-store systems, and because it conforms to the Association of Retail Trading Standards (ARTS), it will integrate with any other ARTS-compliant software.

A systems analyst is needed to determine what is done now by the organization, and what procedures it uses. The systems analyst will analyse the organization as a system and study its inputs, the processes it performs on the inputs, and the outputs. Some of the inputs will be information in one form or another, while other inputs will be more tangible, such as raw materials or products.

The systems analyst will collect a complete set of all manual pro-forma paperwork used for purchasing, invoicing, production and any other purposes. These are important indicators of how the organization functions. Procedures manuals and information system documentation are also useful guides to what was intended should be done. Interviews with staff will establish just how well the procedures manuals correspond with what is actually done in practice, and the reasons for the departure from standard practice. The kinds of skill required here are interviewing skills and an understanding of business procedures, paperwork systems and computer systems.

The last phase of the business analysis, that of establishing what should be done and how, relates to the two previous phases. Procedures should relate directly to the corporate objectives and philosophy. However, in the interest of keeping change to a minimum, the best of the present system should be preserved wherever possible.

This phase requires some technical knowledge as well as business analysis skills. It may be necessary to start making initial contacts with manufacturers and suppliers of systems at this stage. It will be necessary to second more team members in order to bring together for this stage a sufficiently broad spectrum of skills and knowledge in the project team. As a rough guide, it would not be unusual for the business analysis stage of the project to consume a fifth of the total team man-hours over the life of the project.

We have called this stage business analysis: in fact it is often referred to as systems analysis because the business is analysed as a system, and then the systems the business uses – and could use – are analysed. It requires some knowledge of the technology that is available and lays the groundwork for the next stage of the project, the systems design.

Systems design

All the investigation work has now been completed and the results should be available as the 'deliverables' from the business analysis stage, in the form of reports and documentation. These then form the basis for drawing up a full technical specification. If possible, it should not be hardware specific, so that different manufacturers and suppliers can be invited to tender against the specification.

When the steering committee gives the go-ahead for this stage, the project will gain further momentum, using perhaps a third of the total team-hours during the life of the project. The team will grow as some initial input from programmers and engineers will be required.

As well as hardware, software will be needed, which may consist of proven off-the-shelf packages, but for larger applications it is probable that at least some of the software will have to be written specially. The software will not be bought in or written until the next stage, that of implementation, but to prepare the way systems software specifications must be drawn up.

Implementation

This is the major part of the project and it is when the largest expenditure occurs. Half the total project team-hours may be used at this stage, and there will be large capital costs for hardware and software. Also, there will be training costs, which typically may be similar in size to the hardware costs.

This is also the stage at which the major risks occur. Up to this point, there has been no interference with the basic procedures that the organization uses to conduct its affairs. But now it is planned to transfer operations to the new system. Inevitably there will be a 'J-curve' effect where output dips during and immediately after the transfer (Figure 5.4). This must be expected, but if all goes well output should quickly recover to a new higher level, and this too must be anticipated by making sure inputs are adequate to sustain the new higher level of output.

The big risk, of course, is that all may not go well, and the steering committee must be very confident that the system will work. They may require the project team to confirm that all is well before authorizing transfer of operations to the new system.

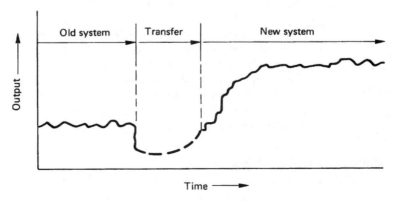

Figure 5.4   *The output 'J-curve'*

The main phases of implementation are:

- Hardware purchase and installation.
- Software purchase and writing.
- Systems and software testing.
- User training.
- File conversion and transfer to the new system.
- Switch to the new system and stop using the old system.

Hardware purchase and installation

This will involve inviting suppliers to tender against the technical specification, but inevitably suppliers will emphasize their strengths, and not dwell on the short-comings of their tender. The project team must make sure that no important areas of weakness are overlooked.

Installation is bound to cause some disruption as ceiling panels are taken down and floors lifted to install communications cabling.

Software purchase and writing

Comparing and assessing the suitability of different packages is quite a complex business. Technical conformance to the specification is obviously important, but the user-friendliness of the human–computer interface is extremely important. The computer experts, because of their familiarity with the way computers work, are sometimes unaware of the difficulties new users have with new systems. These difficulties can be overcome by training, but an inherently difficult system will cause irritation from the start and will never endear itself to the users.

Even standard off-the-shelf software must be installed on the hardware and set up to produce the type of output required. However, users are not always able to describe exactly the type of support they require from the system, until they start using it. Then, they can recognize it when they see it.

In these circumstances, prototyping is appropriate. The programmer uses a fourth-generation programming language, a 4GL, to produce very quickly a limited package with keyboard inputs and screen outputs which can easily be changed. Then, when the user is satisfied, the programmer can go away and write the full version. This will take longer to do than the prototype version, but will have adequate speed and capacity to meet the design specification.

Systems and software testing

When the hardware and software for all the component subsystems have been installed and tested, the whole system, including all computerized and manual procedures, must be tested to ensure it operates in an integrated fashion.

In a big systems project, testing can never guarantee perfection because of the almost infinite number of multiple interrelationships that can arise between program modules. However, common human and physical failures can be anticipated, and so these are purposely introduced. During a test run, erroneous transactions are processed and hardware failures are simulated to check that the system can handle the problem and recover from the failure.

User training

Skimping on training is a false economy, and yet if the project budget is under pressure training is more likely to be cut than hardware. The technology cannot work without people: people form the most important part of the total system.

The trouble lies deep in management attitudes which are reinforced by our financial accounting conventions. Hardware appears as assets on the balance sheet, whereas people don't, so despite claims from the top that 'people are our most important asset', training is not seen as an investment. The government does not help either; they award much more money in grants for equipment than they do for training.

Also, hardware cannot walk away, whereas people can. A typical British manager's attitude is that if you give people training, they are sure to leave because they can use it to secure a better job. This is in stark contrast to the experience of Nissan who have big budgets for on-going training. They know that people will actually decide to stay with them because there are opportunities for training, rather than move and get stuck in a job where there is no training. When Nissan opened a plant in Tennessee, USA, they spent $30,000 per employee on training before the plant started operation.

If money spent on training is not money down the drain, then what is the payoff? There's the rub: the benefits are very difficult to estimate, even with specific operator training. The costs of training are up-front and known exactly, but how can you ever know whether it was worthwhile? All you can do is rely on the advice of consultants with experience of systems projects where greater and lesser amounts were spent on training. They should be able to estimate the savings that arise from shorter start-up and improved system effectiveness.

The documentation produced during the analysis and design stages of the project will provide a rich source of training material.

File conversion and transfer

The files of standing data used by the old system must be copied over to the new system before the new system can operate. For instance, the file of customer addresses and the file of product prices are needed before the system can produce invoices. It is seldom as simple as loading a tape from the old system and getting the new system to read it. Usually the new hardware and software will be incompatible with the old, and special programs will have to be written to translate the old tapes into a form that is understandable by the new system.

If a manual procedure used as part of the previous system is to be computerized, then any necessary manual data will need to be keyed in manually.

The transfer of files must not take too long, however, because life goes on during the transfer and the old system will continue to be used for business until the final switch-over. Thus the state of play on the old system will advance, and the taped data put into the new system will soon be out of date. This will make switching over to the new system difficult because it is not up to date.

Switching to the new system and stopping the old system

Wherever possible a phased implementation should be adopted, with different subsystems brought on-line one at a time. Thus the accounts module could be implemented and tested first, say. Then, when this is operating correctly, the production module could be brought on-line. However, with big real-time systems which rely on a single database – an airline ticket reservation system for instance – it is not possible to reduce the risks in this way: the whole system must be started at the same time.

Severn Trent consults Oracle

Client-server systems allow fast, phased implementation

Severn Trent Water was dominated by mainframe systems until 1996 when they moved payroll processing off the mainframe. Payroll now runs on a client-server system of Hewlett-Packard hardware and Oracle software.

Finance Director Mark Wilson explained: 'The cost of operating the old system was increasing due to the level of support and time required to make changes.'

Wilson was very impressed by the speed of implementation, which took less than six months, and explained that they wanted to test the client-server approach before replacing other systems. The move is part of a £1million project which will also involve the transfer, by 1997, of finance and human resources onto similar client-server systems.

(Source: Computing, 4 July 1996. VNU Business Publications Ltd.

Another way to reduce the risks is to use a period of parallel operation as a safeguard to check that the new system is functioning correctly, before switching off the old system. This should be for a strictly limited period, because maintaining both systems doubles the workload for the users with every transaction having to be input twice. Also, it prevents the users from gaining confidence in the new system. With both systems running, users will revert to the old system whenever there is a difficulty.

The project team should encourage ownership of the system by the users, and should reduce support to normal maintenance levels soon after the old system is abandoned.

Maintenance

This is included as one of the stages in the life cycle of the system, but it is not part of the project because it will last for years, up to the time when a new feasibility study marks the beginning of the next systems project (Figure 5.5).

The purpose of system maintenance is not to maintain the *status quo*, like car maintenance for instance. Maintenance in the context of information systems means maintaining a system which is appropriate to the business needs of the organization. There will be occasions when a system 'bug' requires fixing, but for the most part maintenance is more a question of adjusting the system to suit the changing needs of the organization over time.

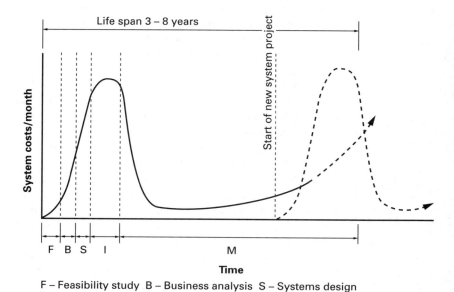

F – Feasibility study B – Business analysis S – Systems design
I – Implementation M – Maintenance

Figure 5.5 *Bathtub curve of system lifetime costs*

A change in the rate for value added tax (VAT) is one example of the kind of influence that may result in a need for system maintenance. The program that computes the amount of VAT charged on invoices will need to be edited.

One of the project team's last responsibilities is to conduct a post-implementation review. The purpose of this is to compare the performance of the system with what was originally specified in the systems design documentation. As a result, before finally being disbanded, the team may be asked by users to do some post-implementation fine-tuning of the system.

Apart from acting as an important control activity, the post-implementation review is a valuable opportunity for team members to learn from the experience of being involved with the project. It will add to their value as team members on the next project.

ORACLE at work

Testing the ORACLE

Test Valley Borough Council's housing department is reaching the end of an extensive software development which will provide the department programme with a comprehensive system for maintenance and rent collection.

John Spens, principal assistant chief housing officer at Test Valley, appointed a small working party at the end of 1989 to investigate the software packages currently on the market but, after four months, concluded that there was nothing suitable for his housing department. 'Our primary criterion was excellence, but, like all local councils, we needed to find a cost-effective solution.'

'We visited several other councils to discuss the solutions that they had implemented, but this failed to turn up anything suitable for our purposes.' Currently, all thirteen authorities in Hampshire have different systems in place.

Test Valley is replacing two separate systems with a single integrated solution; a 15-year-old rent system which was originally jointly developed for Test Valley and Winchester City Council, and DILIS, a maintenance system purchased from ICL in 1984. The council properties to be included are all houses, flats and garages in the council's ownership, as well as properties which are on short-term leases.

Spens' next step was to arrange for an initial specification of the system to be prepared. This was then sent to five different software houses including ORACLE and PIC. 'As a housing department we had little previous experience of Oracle and invited them to tender on the strength of the company's reputation and recommendations received from other users', said Spens.

'PIC and Oracle decided to offer a joint bid which was excellent news for us, as it meant combining PIC's extensive expertise in housing with Oracle's strength in IT as a leading software company', said Spens.

The Oracle/PIC bid was accepted by Test Valley Borough Council in September 1990 and the companies started work on developing a complete turnkey system for the department.

Using Oracle's CASE methodology the development team started with three months of analysis in defining the scope of the system. 'Although we had supplied quite a detailed specification there was a lot of fine detail to be decided', explained Spens.

Around ten users at Test Valley were involved in this analysis stage. In addition to Spens and the project manager, the other users came from various sections of the Housing Department, such as Rent Arrears, Rent Accounting, Estate Management, Responsive Maintenance and Programmed Maintenance.

'Initially, the users were rather sceptical about the system, but they were soon won over as they found how much power to influence the system lay in their hands', explained Peter Bird, the project manager. 'Very often users are simply handed a system with little previous consultation and told to get on with it.'

'The CASE methodology was extremely useful in building confidence levels. Using the diagramming techniques all the users were able to understand the scope and direction the system was taking and a lot of valuable feedback was gleaned in the early stages.'

Context sensitive help

'We have put a high priority on making the system as intuitive and easy to use as possible. Additionally there is a large degree of context sensitive help available to users on line which has also allayed many of their fears', Bird continued.

Time scales were fairly tight and Spens had set dates of July 1991 for the rents. 'We decided to give council tenants a rent free week at the end of September as there are 53 Mondays this year, and this would help smooth the transition between the old and the new systems.'

At present everything is on line for these targets and the project is currently in the build phase with an accompanying increase in activity. There is a total of 23 people working on the project, with up to six Oracle consultants on site at any one time. Users have also been actively involved in running acceptance testing.

'There will be forty-two terminals in the department which will be connected to the system giving almost all staff desktop access', said Bird.

Intensive training

Intensive training is planned during June for all users, and the systems will be run in tandem for two weeks in order to ensure data integrity and that there are no hiccups in going live.

The system will include approximately 100 modules and can be divided into three areas: estate management, repairs and rent. The estate management segment keeps all details of properties, which includes statistical information on accommodation, number of bedrooms, garden sizes and many other attributes useful for repairs such as window frames, roof tiles, plumbing and central heating. Much of the information to fill this database will be transferred from the current system. Whenever repair orders are issued and completed, attributes are automatically changed so that information is always up-to-date.

The second segment deals with repairs and provides the complete system for inputting and managing 40,000 repair jobs every year. The system holds a schedule of rates for different jobs so that the best contractors can be selected for each repair task. Details of when jobs are issued, to whom and what priority rating they have been assigned are also included.

'We are expecting a big improvement in service to our customers as management information will be far better. The system will supply us with details on how reliable contractors are, how many jobs each has been issued with, whether targets are being met and where any hold-ups are occurring.'

The third and final part deals with rents and will handle the rental income of £11 million per annum and will particularly assist with the recovery of rent arrears.

'Rent assistants will have access to complete and up-to-date records of rent payments and will be able to select one of twenty different standard letters held on file. These are automatically generated but can be tailored or personalized if appropriate. Additionally, we will be able to generate statements of account on demand with a few keystrokes. These will include all payments, details of housing benefit, credits and debits.'

The computer will play an important role in monitoring arrangements for reducing rent arrears and individual schedules for payment. The system will alert the department if there is a deviation from the agreed payment plan. Another useful feature is the system's calendar which keeps a note of when Notice of Seeking Possessions are issued and will alert the department when they are due to expire.

'Test Valley has a good record on rent arrears anyway', admits Spens, 'but now it should be even better.' A lot of attention was devoted to the design of the system so that it will interface perfectly with other systems which are renewed or replaced in the future.

Five-year payback

Spens estimates that the system will pay for itself within five years on a straight financial basis, without considering the improved service and efficiency. 'There were very high costs associated with running DILIS on the Council's mainframe. ICL DRS 6000 hardware with ORACLE is a far more cost effective solution.'

'As well as the financial justification there are a number of other benefits, which we will gain,' explained Spens. 'Firstly, the system will be completely up-to-date with a very high degree of applicability, financial and management information. It will be far easier to access and reports can be generated either on an ad hoc basis or as standard, planning and budgetary control will be vastly improved and many of the tasks that could previously only be achieved after hours of manual work can be completed in a matter of minutes.'

As far as the system's life cycle is concerned, Spens admits that it is virtually impossible to predict this, but he confidently expects the ORACLE system to withstand the next 15 years at least: 'Rent accounting has hardly changed over the past decade. However, one can't predict legislative changes and "future-proofing" is important.'

'We are very optimistic about the improvements that the new integrated system will bring and feel confident about the decision we have made', concluded Spens.

Object-oriented systems

There is a new development on the horizon that you should know about, which could eventually make redundant the meticulous systems analysis and planning we've just reviewed. Objects have been used by computer scientists for decades, mostly for research in artificial intelligence, but are now being used to construct business information systems. Objects are software modules consisting of part procedures and part data, which represent real-world business objects such as products, customers, orders and accounts. Objects can therefore be used to model the way a business works, and to build a system to manage the business.

Current system development projects require meticulous planning because conventional programming results in a single monolithic system with a basic architecture which, once put together, is almost impossible to alter. Of course, a business information system must reflect the organizational structure of the business it serves, and if a change in the environment demands a change in the organization, the information system will need to be changed too. A rigid, monolithic and hideously expensive information system written in conventional code can lock an organization into a particular mode of operating. This can be bad news if an organization needs to restructure to respond to a rapidly changing business environment.

Objects, however, are like Lego bricks that can be clipped together to build a system – then pulled apart and rebuilt to a new architecture if necessary – which makes it much easier for the organization to restructure in response to changing business needs. Object-oriented systems are also much quicker and cheaper to develop and maintain. It is claimed that such systems can be developed between twice and ten times as fast as conventional systems.

This sounds like excellent news, but there are heavy up-front costs and long lead-times for learning and benefiting from the new programming methods. Also, there is that old bugbear of standards. To benefit fully, users should be able to buy and sell objects, or even rent them over the Internet, but this will only be possible when one of the several standards in use emerges as the industry standard. Meanwhile, the risks and costs will inhibit many from adopting this potentially attractive new approach.

However, despite the risks and costs, object-oriented systems seem to be fundamentally suited to the new business imperatives. Businesses are urgently seeking a more flexible alternative to industrial-age hierarchy and centralized command and control as a way of organizing. The fast-moving information age calls for speed of response which only a team of small, empowered teams can achieve. The question today is not how to retain control at the top, but how to co-ordinate teams with devolved responsibility for projects and processes. In Chapter 2 we saw how R. N. Anthony's organization is being replaced by Tom Peters' model. We need new systems for new ways of working. Thus the triad of hierarchy, the mainframe and the central database looks threatened by a new triad: team-of-teams, client-server networks and distributed objects. How soon, if ever, will object-oriented systems be rolled out in your organization? Only time will tell.

In the next chapter, we will examine some recent developments in computer networks which seem set to create a global electronic marketplace with new business opportunities and threats. We will identify the trends, and try to guess where they will lead.

Competence self-assessment

1   List the five stages in the life cycle of a management information system project. Write a couple of lines describing the purpose of each stage. Sketch a graph to show how cost and effectiveness vary over the life of a system.

2   Describe the membership of the project team. What skills are required, and at which stages are the different skills required? When should system users be involved?

3   What are the advantages and disadvantages of employing external consultants on a systems project?

4   Describe the organizational structure, and procedures for the overall control of the project. When do the major risks and costs occur, and how are they monitored and controlled?

5   Describe how computers first came to be used for business purposes. What tasks where they used for then? What distinct stages can you identify in the increasing business use of computers over the last forty years? What problems have arisen from this development, and how might they be overcome?

6   What is meant by the principle of single data entry for multiple users? Why is it thought to be important in the design of management information systems?

7   What are the three main areas of investigation in a business analysis conducted as part of a systems project? Briefly describe the sources that should be examined in these three areas.

8   List the six major tasks that make up the implementation stage of a systems project. Write a couple of lines to describe the purpose of each task.

References and further reading

Curtis, G. (1995). *Business Information Systems – Analysis, Design and Practice* (2nd edition). Addison Wesley.

Wilson, D. A. (1996). *Managing Knowledge*. Butterworth-Heinemann, Institute of Marketing.

Curtis, a British author, provides a very comprehensive academic review of information systems. The book doesn't have the many colour illustrations contained in many American texts. However, it starts the topics from a simple level that most readers will be able to handle, and develops them to a technical level advanced enough for all but the most knowledgeable manager.

Wilson's book, the sequel to *Managing Information*, assumes that, as most business resources are in surplus and get cheaper every year, the only sustainable basis for competition is superior knowledge. The book examines how to exploit the knowledge resource fully, without exploiting people. It describes how to use networks, teams, projects and computers in order to replace command-and-control where knowledge is suppressed, with inform-and-entrust where it flourishes.

6 Information around the world and into the future

Why is this chapter relevant?

This chapter looks beyond today and the immediate boundaries of your organization, to see where the current trends are leading. Falling costs, greater power, easier access and smaller size, coupled with multimedia, wireless communications and the Internet – the trends are so firmly established they must sooner or later reach a critical threshold. What new commercial possibilities lie waiting, and how will they affect your organization?

Meanwhile, global networks are already changing the ways we do business, opening up new opportunities for electronic commerce, and presenting new threats. Are you prepared for this important development? Perhaps you are already affected. However, this chapter should provide the background to press coverage of the Internet and the new things computers can do. The implications of the stories as they break, should then be clearer both for you and your organization.

Information and the global marketplace

Kenichi Ohmae is the managing director in Japan of the international management consultants McKinsey & Co. In his book *The Borderless World*, Ohmae, who is one of the leading writers on corporate planning, is concerned that too few managers are developing truly global strategies.

'On a political map, the boundaries between countries are as clear as ever. But', says Ohmae, 'on a competitive map, a map showing the real flows of financial and industrial activity, those boundaries have largely disappeared. Of all the forces eating them away, perhaps the most persistent is the flow of information.'

We are becoming global citizens. Turn on your TV and you will see shots of people in the streets of Singapore, Moscow, Baghdad, Tokyo, Hong Kong, Paris, New York . . . We can all see for ourselves people in the streets of cities all around the world. We see their choice of clothes, the cars they drive – their preferences in fashion, sports and lifestyles. And news reporters always seem to be able to find someone who speaks English, because it seems English is becoming the common language of the global citizen.

Within big corporations, this globalization is even more advanced. Executives dress the same, use similar offices and equipment, drive similar cars, operate similar machines – and mostly speak English. This makes it easy for executives to switch corporations and switch countries.

Ohmae believes that 'When information flows with freedom, the old geographic barriers become irrelevant. Global needs lead to global products. For managers, this flow of information puts a high premium on learning how to build the strategies and the organizations capable of meeting the requirements of a borderless world.' These observations are, of course, even more true now than when Ohmae made them, as a direct result of burgeoning public interest in the Internet. Myopic managers with limited, parochial ambitions will lose out in this new global marketplace.

Global networks

It is easy for us to observe information in the public domain such as TV news stories, but many people are unaware of the volume of private information flowing unobserved between countries and ignoring national boundaries. The volume of these rising streams of digitally coded information is growing rapidly, roughly doubling every six years.

Private information flows mostly through private international networks, set up for specific purposes. For instance, the world's major banks belong to a private network, the Society for World-wide Interbank Financial Transactions (SWIFT), which allows subscribers to make a transaction half way round the world and have it acknowledged within a few seconds. The system handles transactions worth hundreds of billions of pounds on a typical day, and this is just one network amongst several others serving the banking sector, such as the Clearing House for International Payments (CHIPS) and the Clearing House Automated Payment System (CHAPS).

There are hundreds of other private networks to handle all manner of different information types. There are networks for electronic mail, for electronic commerce and electronic data interchange (EDI), for airline seat reservations, for meteorological data, for international news services, and for the export of information services – to name but a few.

Generally the networks are constructed around mainframe databases, with remote access and file transfer available through a network of leased lines, satellite links and submarine cables operated by bulk carriers. The older networks are based around traditional telephone technology, but the newer networks are digital, offering much greater capacity, accuracy and speed.

In the UK, network operators offer their services through British Telecom or Mercury transmission lines. Both have two different types of line: the old telephone wire lines which are designed for speech, and the new Integrated Services Digital Network (ISDN) which makes use of fibre optic cables to carry not only digitally coded text and graphics but also voice and moving video.

Desktop video conferencing

NEC links America and Japan by desktop video conferencing

Figure 6.1 *A MERMAID desktop video conferencing system (courtesy of NEC Corporation)*

In 1992, NEC Corporation developed an international teleconferencing system, based on a network of special workstations which incorporated a small television camera (Figure 6.1). Users on the network had access to a central database and could communicate with each other in real-time by voice and video pictures, while sharing a joint view of their work in the form of text, graphics, scanned images and hand drawings.

NEC's system, called MERMAID, made it possible for people on different continents to work as a team, vocally interacting in real-time while sharing a common view of their work as it developed. NEC used the system between their headquarters in Tokyo and four research centres – three in Japan and one in America. All of this was achieved before roll-out of the World Wide Web, the multimedia enhancement of Internet; thus, in order to make the system possible, NEC scientists had to develop their own multimedia communications protocol, for use on ISDN and other computer networks, including the Internet.

MERMAID, which stands for Multimedia Environment for Remote Multi-attendee Interactive Decision-making, allows real-time international group work between a number of participants from anywhere in the world wherever there is a workstation linked to the network. It is an example of equipment designed for computer supported co-operative work (CSCW), such as:

- Co-operative software development.
- Group decision support.
- Interactive education and training.
- Financial trading support.
- Joint authoring and document editing.
- Home working.
- Remote information retrieval from multimedia databases.

By 1996, there were several companies in the West offering desktop video conferencing on modest 486/16MB PCs. However, even though they require an ISDN2 connection via British Telecom, few can offer better than 15 frames per second, although some can offer TV quality 30 fps by using three parallel ISDN2 connections. Suppliers include BT, Picturetel, VTEL and Creative Labs.

If you have a multimedia PC with a modem to the Internet, you can get video conferencing of sorts for a mere £169, which will buy you the software and a monochrome video camera from CU-SeeMe. However, performance will be dubious at busy times on the Internet.

Clearly there is huge business potential in video conferencing, and new developments are arriving thick and fast. By the time you read this, further developments may already have occurred.

Electronic commerce and electronic data interchange

EDI is a generic term used to describe networks set up between purchasing organizations and their suppliers, to speed up the process of making enquiries, placing orders, invoicing and settling accounts. The original idea was to get rid of the paperwork by taking the digital purchasing information from the purchaser's computer, and inputting it directly into the supplier's computer. EDI was expected to be cheaper, faster and less prone to typographical errors. However, not only did EDI save clerical costs, it also allowed suppliers to deliver materials at the same rate at which they were consumed. It allowed just-in-time deliveries, cutting out work-in-progress and thus enabling greater flexibility and higher quality production.

EDI drives the Rover 220 at Longbridge

Rover keep inventory to an absolute minimum at Longbridge by using just-in-time deliveries, and schedules sent automatically to suppliers via AT&T EasyLink EDI. In extreme cases, forty minutes is all it takes to schedule and deliver critical parts for the Rover 220 Coupe, but usually suppliers have between twelve hours and one week's notice.

There are schedules for 'timed delivery' and 'sequenced delivery'. Timed delivery works on a weekly basis, but sequenced delivery works round the clock, sometimes every two hours, to ensure you don't get red wing mirrors on your metallic blue coupé. Bar codes are fixed to the body shells as they go on the track, which a PC scans and translates to an EDI message sent to the supplier for parts needed usually twelve or thirteen hours further down the track. Colour co-ordinated wing mirrors, however, are scheduled after the paint plant, just forty minutes ahead of 'trim & final'.

EDI is the reliable, utilitarian, unglamorous side of networking. It has been around in the UK since the 1980s and has quietly been maturing, expanding and saving users millions of pounds every year. For instance, in 1990 British Coal held stocks of 200,000 different products to support their operations, sent out 600,000 purchase orders and received 1.6 million invoices every year. But even then they had EDI links with 500 different suppliers, and one-third of their orders – 200,000 of them – were placed electronically. Shorter lead-times between placing orders and receiving goods allowed reduced stock levels, which released £1 million, and lower administration costs saved a further £50,000 each year.

For computers to be able to exchange messages the 'protocols' – that is the language, codes and routines for the exchange – must be agreed. Setting up direct communications between computers used to be quite tricky in the early days of EDI, because there were many different languages, codes and routines in use, and if the protocol used by the receiving computer differed even in the tiniest way from that used by the transmitting computer, then communications could not be established.

Communications were easiest to implement if both trading partners had the same hardware and software. The digital data could then be transferred by direct communications link, or by physical exchange of tapes or disks. However, it was rare for trading partners to find they had exactly the same systems.

As the benefits of EDI caught on, more organizations wanted to join in, but usually they had incompatible systems. The original parties would already have an agreed data format for the exchange, and so newcomers would then have to convert their data to that format before it would be possible to communicate.

This was an unsatisfactory situation, and soon third-party network operators stepped in to act as electronic clearing houses between groups of purchasers and groups of suppliers. Different network operators focused on the needs of particular industries, and performed a valuable service in setting standards for each industry. They became known as value added network service suppliers, or VANs for short.

The VAN service consists of a computer database between the customer and supplier, which allows each company to have its own electronic mailbox through which it can send and receive commercial messages such as orders and invoices. Thus, before sending off a message, a company must first translate it into the format required by the VAN computer.

On receiving the message, the VAN service reads the address and places it in the intended recipient's mailbox. The recipient then downloads the message from the VAN service into its own internal computer system, but before they can be used the data must again be translated, from the VAN format into the format required by the recipient's computer system. The software for communicating with the VAN computer is supplied by the operator of the service, and once set up messages can pass through the service almost instantaneously.

The four main EDI VAN networks in the UK are:

- GEIS who offer Tradanet and EDI*Exchange.
- IBM who offer Global Network Services.
- AT&T who offer EasyLink.
- BT who offer EDI*Net.

These four global network providers are 'closed', or private, networks managed by the operators and available only to subscribers, in contrast to the Internet which is not managed (but operates to agreed standards) and is open to anyone. The VAN operators guarantee delivery, integrity and security – features which are valued highly by their customers.

GEIS, part of General Electric Company in America, established a major presence in the UK by purchasing INS, a UK service originally set up by ICL. GEIS serves the retail and distribution, pharmaceuticals, automotive and several other sectors. IBM serves the insurance, health and many other sectors, and these two companies between them carry well over half the EDI messages in the UK. The rest are carried by AT&T, plus BT and other smaller providers. Like GEIS, AT&T also gained market share by purchasing a British company – Istel, formed when British Leyland sold off its information system division.

EROS at Virgin Megastores

Over the Christmas period, Virgin Megastores take 20 per cent of their annual sales in just five weeks, employing 200 staff at Oxford Street alone. All 300 stores (and another 400 UK retailers) use EROS – an EDI system from AT&T for checking catalogue details and ordering new releases in music, video and games. Staff take less than two minutes on-screen to check the product, enter and send an order.

Every week about 700 changes to the catalogue are broadcast to retailers' EasyLink mailboxes. The Megastores' catalogues are always up-to-date because the next time an order is placed, the changes are automatically loaded onto their PCs.

The UK is well ahead of Europe in using EDI. Most, if not all, of *The Times* Top 100 companies use EDI, and about two-thirds of all European EDI activity is here in the UK. As users in world markets, the UK is second only to the USA.

However, our lead has resulted in a plethora of incompatible systems. Served by the four main VAN operators in the UK there are several industrial groups who have agreed messaging standards for electronic trading. For instance:

● CEFIC in the chemical industry.
● EDIFICE in the electronics industry.
● ODETTE in the automotive industry.
● EDICON in the construction industry.

World-wide, however, there are three leading standards:

● In the UK it is the TRADACOMS (Trading Data Communications) standard, as they have the biggest customer base of over 2000 users.
● In the USA it is ANSI ASC X.12 (American National Standards Institute).
● Internationally, it is EDIFACT (Electronic Data Interchange for Administration, Commerce and Transport). This was established in 1985, and by 1991 had only developed standards for one message type, the purchase order, compared to TRADACOMS' sixteen standards. Securing international agreement takes time, but EDIFACT has received wide endorsement from companies and governments around the world, who all accept that there is no future for local or national standards in the global marketplace.

A decade of consolidation has led to the four main providers, who have developed bridges to allow interoperability between the different

EDI networks. However, complaints are still heard from the small to medium sized enterprises, that EDI is a big company club. Small companies find it difficult to justify the entry cost charged by the VAN operators, currently reaching into the thousands of pounds. However, rapid developments in the Internet are opening up new possibilities. Companies can already exchange e-mail messages, and so messages conforming to EDI formats are already technically possible. Software is being developed to guarantee security, delivery and integrity. EDI over the Internet will then be possible without a VAN operator in between, and at a cost of only hundreds rather than thousands of pounds.

The VAN operators are unlikely to suffer mass customer desertions, but they would like a share of this market. GEIS for instance is offering GE TradeWeb, a forms-based, entry-level EDI service presented as a Web page. Using a browser, a company can fill out ready-to-use EDI forms such as purchase orders, invoices and acknowledgements. TradeWeb then translates the forms into the EDI protocols necessary to deliver them to large VAN customers.

The Internet has opened up a whole new range of commercial possibilities, but in doing so, it has made the formerly rather staid EDI market much less predictable.

The Internet

The Internet is an amazing phenomenon which seems to have burst onto the scene from nowhere, but in fact its origins can be traced back a quarter of a century, to a network set up in the USA by the Advanced Projects Research Agency, to serve scientists working on Department of Defense projects. This small network grew and linked with other networks, at first just in the USA, but later world-wide after the Defense Agency relinquished control.

Recent developments made the Internet easily accessible to the general public, and suddenly the world woke up to the business potential of this network of networks. It is growing astonishingly fast, attracting millions of new users annually, and offering new developments almost daily. To try to understand the Internet, let's start with a look at its history and architecture. Then we can look at some current ways in which it is being used, and by projecting the trends perhaps guess at possible opportunities and threats the Internet may present for business today and in the future.

History and architecture

I remember being asked in the 1980s, whether I would use Janet, the Joint Academic Network, if our institution were to connect into it. Janet consisted of university mainframes in the UK, linked to their neighbours by permanent telecommunications lines. This network was set up to allow academics at any UK university to exchange files and messages with academics anywhere else in the network. Screens were monochrome, files were just text and numbers, and to use the system you needed to know Unix, an operating system consisting of mysterious codes and arcane keyboard commands. As you can imagine, it was not used much by staff outside of the science and technology departments. I didn't think I'd use it much.

In the USA, similar computer networks had been established. They were funded by the Department of Defense to assist researchers working on military contracts, who were often separated by the much greater distances in North America. Eventually, the USA and UK networks were linked, and other countries also connected up. The Internet is thus a network of networks, which operates without any centralized control, other than agreeing to the same TCP/IP communications protocols – the initials stand for transmission control protocol/internet protocol, the name for the set of open, non-proprietary conventions which underpin the remarkable robustness of the Internet.

TCP/IP requires a communication to be split into 'packets', each with its own address so they can be routed individually through the network. The originating computer then sends them off, looking each time for a line to another computer in the network nearer to the packet's destination address. If a line is busy or otherwise unavailable, the computer will send the packet via the next available line going in the right general direction. Packets get passed from computer to computer through the network, with the packets of a message perhaps taking different paths to their destination. On arrival they are re-assembled in their correct order.

It is often said that the network was designed this way so it could still function with large parts of it knocked out by a nuclear attack. However, in the 1960s computers were slower and less reliable, and the switched packet solution was probably chosen as the only practical way of ensuring messages got through.

Thus the foundations were laid, but for many years the superstructure remained user-unfriendly, and the content unattractive to most people except a few computer scientists and researchers. Then suddenly around 1993, three enhancements were added which transformed the Internet into an easy, exciting point-and-click environment, attractive and accessible to almost anyone. They were Windows, hypertext and multimedia. The birth of the World Wide Web was hot news, and it ignited public and commercial interest.

However, at the end of 1996 few organizations except those selling access and web space were generating direct, tangible earnings from the Internet. Companies were constructing shop windows in cyberspace in the form of home pages which net surfers could visit, and there was intense competition to write the most functional and user-friendly World Wide Web browser. Teams of software writers at Microsoft burned the midnight oil to bring out frequent new versions

The Internet grows up

(Please refer to the glossary for any terms you don't understand.)

1969	ARPANET formed	An ARPA-controlled network of university, military and defence contractors, to aid researchers in sharing information. It allowed remote log-on, file transfer and e-mail.
1973	Internetting project	A DARPA project to study how to link packet networks together.
1974	TCP/IP developed	A system of protocols developed for wide area networking.
1980	CSNET allowed to connect to the ARPANET	CSNET – for linking university computer science departments in several states. The first autonomous network DARPA allowed to connect to ARPANET.
1983	ARPANET split into MILNET and ARPANET	ARPANET for research into networking. MILNET for military communications.
1985	100 networks now linked	
1989	CSNET merges with BITNET	BITNET – a network for academic discussion between faculty members of all disciplines at universities.
1990	ARPANET decommissioned:	Commercial networks allowed to link. 2200 networks linked
1991	4000 networks linked	
1993	11,000 networks linked	Internet in 100 different countries. 10 million users.
1995		40 million users.
1998		100 million users anticipated.

of Internet Explorer, while similar teams at Netscape were doing the same with Navigator. And as they competed for pole position in the market, both browsers were offered free of charge to users.

Clearly there is great commercial potential in this new medium, but we have yet to discover the best ways to exploit it. The academic origins of the Internet have left a strong anti-commercial culture, with traditions of information being given freely, which along with the highly competitive environment, are making it difficult for businesses to charge for services. There are also dangers in an unregulated and mostly unregulatable global environment which reflects every aspect of human experience – from the inspired to the idiotic, and from the divine to the obscene. Companies are concerned about security. They are building firewalls to insulate their internal networks from attack through the Internet, and searching for secure ways of making and receiving payments over the Internet. Perhaps when these problems are solved, the profits will start to flow.

Present uses

To get access to the Internet, you must either operate a mainframe at one of the nodes in the network, or you must buy access to one, usually with a PC connected via a dial-up or rented telecommunications line. There are lots of companies which make a business out of providing Internet access, and they are known as independent service providers, or ISPs. The minimum service they provide for their customers, the users, consists of:

- An e-mail address, to allow messaging with other users linked to the Internet.
- Web space on the mainframe, on which to build your own web site.
- Help line and software for e-mail, browsing, file transfer, and remote log-on.

Some big service providers such as CompuServe and Microsoft Net also offer private network services which are only available to their own subscribers, and not the rest of the Internet. These may include electronic magazines (e-zines), research databases, bulletin boards, computer games, and facilities for booking airline tickets, hire cars and hotel reservations. Many of these compete with similar facilities on the Internet.

In 1996 the main uses for the Internet could be grouped as follows:

- E-mail.
- Advertising and promotion.
- Bulletin boards and forums.
- Publications.
- On-line shopping.
- Information for sale.
- Free information.

E-mail has a future. You can send a message several pages long half way round the world for the price of a local telephone call. That on its own is a cost advantage, and your message is delivered almost instantly. Also, if you have the right equipment, at no extra cost you can attach colour pictures, and sound and moving images to be played back, too. However, few of my friends log-on at home, and like the telephone, e-mail will not take off until a critical mass of users is reached.

Advertising and promotion is already a big part of the Internet, but it has particular strengths and weaknesses. For instance, you can find out how many people visit your web site, and their e-mail addresses too. You can get your visitors to interact with your material, perhaps by asking them to tick boxes or answer questions on screen. This can yield valuable instant marketing information. At first sight the medium seems ideally suited to mass direct mailing by e-mail. Technically, 'spamming' as it is called, is so easy and carries no cost to the advertiser, but of course if it became widespread the network would quickly grind to a halt as communications and in-trays became choked with junk e-mail. Thus the culture of Internet, or 'Nettiquette', does not permit spamming, and other users may retaliate by 'flaming' the perpetrator – that is jointly sending many

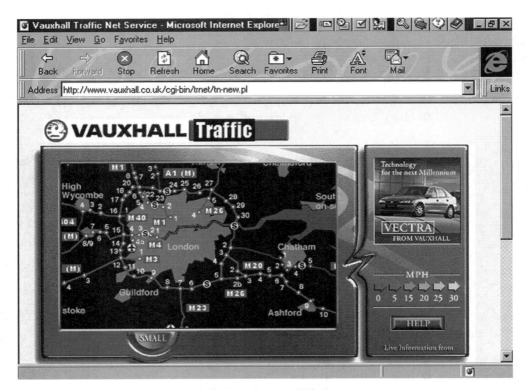

Figure 6.2 *The Vauxhall Motor Company Web site*

Figure 6.3   *The CareerSite Web home page*

thousands of very long and abusive replies in order to overload the spammer's computer.

Advertisers must therefore make their site an interesting place to visit. It costs nothing to change your web site material, or at least there are no direct costs. You can therefore offer information with last-minute accuracy. The Vauxhall Motor Company's Web site is an example (Figure 6.2). It displays maps showing traffic congestion updated from Traffic-Net, which collects information from road-side sensors throughout the UK. It is an example of good Web site design, because people will visit sites where there is useful free information.

A particular weakness of the Internet from the marketing point of view is that currently it tends not to reach so many older people, computerphobes or females. Nevertheless, the Internet can be an excellent medium for matching job seekers with job opportunities in some types of employment. For instance CareerSite invite employers to advertise job opportunities, and job seekers to file their CVs (Figure 6.3). Then profiles can be matched, and users can query the database. There are similar services available at topjobs.co.uk and at worknet.co.uk

Bulletin boards, newsgroups, software user groups and forums for special interest groups proliferate on the Internet, and some of them (less than one per cent) offer material which is pornographic and objectionable. A way of removing such material is needed, and a self-regulatory approach is being developed in the UK between the Internet industry, the police and the courts. The scheme will consist of a voluntary code of conduct, a hotline for reporting breaches, and the co-operation of the ISPs to filter out illegal material. This approach is thought to have a better chance of success than relying just on legal or technical methods, and European ministers seem to agree, as they are likely adopt a similar system for Europe.

The overwhelming majority of user groups perform a useful function. For instance, user groups for commercial software are well established, and often frequented by the programmers who wrote or maintain the software. If you have a technical problem with software you are using, post a message with the user group and you will get lots of suggestions from others who have solved similar problems.

Publications on the Internet fall into two groups: those published first, or only, on the net, and those which are a digital version of the printed version sold on the street. *Slate* is an example of an e-zine, offered by Microsoft, which you can visit at http://www.slate.com. Several of the quality newspapers such as *The Telegraph*, the *Financial Times* and *The Guardian* are available on line, which makes it easy to use your computer to search for articles on a particular subject.

On-line shopping in the form of an electronic mall has been available through CompuServe and other commercial networks for several years, and similar services are beginning to emerge on the Internet despite largely unfounded worries about sending credit card details through the net. You can easily buy your compact discs cheap in America now, but you'll need to order several to defray the shipping costs.

Much information is free on the Internet. It includes weather maps and airline flight departure and arrival times. Free software is also available. However, you often have to pay for some information such as real-time share price movements (at present). To get access, you usually have to pay a monthly or annual subscription.

There is so much information on the Web. The trouble is that with over 30 million Web pages to search, there is a major problem in finding the specific information you require. There are, however, search engines and intelligent agents to help you. AltaVista, Lycos and Yahoo are popular examples of search engines. They require you to enter key words to search for, and they list the addresses where they find them. Then, by clicking on an address in the list, a hypertext link is activated and the file is opened.

Intelligent agents, however, allow natural language requests to be entered. Then you can send them off to roam cyberspace looking for and bringing back files they think might interest you. You can even leave some of them working the net while you disconnect, and you can retrieve them next time you log-on. Web Retriever, More Like This, WebCompass and AutoNomy are current examples of intelligent agents, but at the time of writing there are no clear market leaders.

The best way to find out about Internet is to try it – but be warned: there are interesting distractions at every turn, and you can end up wandering aimlessly. Stay focused, or an hour can slip by in ten minutes.

Future possibilities for the Internet

In 1953, Thomas J. Watson, the president of IBM, predicted the world wouldn't need more than five computers, so we should beware of jumping to conclusions here. However, we can review the main advantages of the Net, and see where these may lead. Also, we can list other separate technological developments which already exist, and which could easily be combined with the Net to produce new products and services. In other words, we can look at what is already technically possible, and see what might happen when already established trends reach some critical level. For instance, we know that hardware prices are falling, that home ownership of personal computers is rising, and that consumer acceptance of the Net is improving.

The advantages of the Net are that it provides a universal standard and infrastructure for multimedia communications. It is also instant, free and easy to use. And it can be used with software to automate routine tasks, such as searching for and presenting useful information. Straight away these advantages suggest the Net may soon become more convenient for looking up information currently available in conventionally published tables and directories. Bus and train timetables, telephone directories and *Yellow Pages* on the Net could all be easier for the user and cheaper for the publisher, with obvious implications for those who currently print these types of material. And how will we search for a new house or car when we want to buy one in the future?

Electronic commerce between companies on the Net also offers a cheap alternative to existing forms of EDI as offered by value-added network service providers. Smaller companies may soon be using EDI, but the VANs are unlikely to win much new business, once the few worries about security on the Net have been cleared up. Compatibility of systems will cease to be an issue, and EDI may soon no longer be dominated by larger companies in exclusive clubs serving particular industries.

New technologies now in existence include wireless connection as used by mobile phones, hand-held computers such as those offered by Psion, mini TV cameras as mounted in the cricket stumps at test matches, and live voice and video sent over networks. The price of all these technologies is falling, and will eventually become cheap

---

NET-CONNECT EDI offers secure Internet messaging

Albany Software of Farnham, Surrey, is a leading UK provider of solutions for electronic trading and commerce. They are also one of the first companies to offer a secure gateway to the Internet for conveying EDI messages, though others are sure to follow. They offer local call connection and make no volume-related subscription charges. For small business EDI users this is likely to be an attractive low-cost alternative to the VAN service providers.

---

enough for consumers to buy on impulse. This will open up new possibilities for integrating these technologies with the Net, which will result in new commercial opportunities, though what they may be we can only guess at. The industries most likely to be affected are the information and communications industries – those which offer telephones, education, banking and financial services, music, news, video, TV, games and entertainment.

What possibilities do you see ahead?

The Data Protection Act 1984

What would you think if you were refused life insurance though perfectly fit? Or inexplicably refused credit? Or failed to get a job because the interviewer somehow knew of your past membership of a political party or trade union? Would you be disturbed, if on responding by phone to an advertisement, you find the salesman knows who you are without being told? Would it upset you if he also knows your age, the credit cards you use, and the fact that you spend most weekends away in Brighton?

You would rightly be outraged and extremely alarmed if you found that details, perhaps erroneous, of your medical, financial and personal life were in general circulation and being used against you. But, technically, this Big Brother scenario is feasible right now, and the only protection you and I as individuals have is the Data Protection Act, which by curious coincidence was passed in 1984.

It has always been possible to use technology for good or evil, and this time it is database technology which we must channel in the right direction. Organizations use databases to keep records of their customers, clients, patients, members, shareholders, students, etc., together with their addresses and details of transactions of various types. Every time you join a professional association, buy shares, fill in a guarantee card or book a holiday, your name and address and details of the transaction are added to a database. On their own these records pose no threat to you, but if they are brought together, cross-referenced and compared, they reveal a detailed picture of your habits and lifestyle which should remain private.

Databases are stored on disk and in computer memory, and the cost per kilobyte of storage has roughly halved every two years since business computers were first used. This phenomenon shows every sign of continuing, and it is now economic to store millions of records, any one of which can be accessed in seconds. An obvious application in this era of the credit card, is the running of instant creditworthiness checks. If you make a large purchase with your Access or Visa card, the salesperson will phone up the credit card company to check the status of your account. It takes seconds for the computer to access your account number from amongst the millions of others.

The world of business has not been slow to see the potential from a marketing point of view. By buying and selling lists of different types and bringing them together into a single database, selective searches can be made to produce lists of potential customers who conform to some desired profile. There is no point trying to sell to a person who hasn't the money or use for your product. For instance suppose you want to sell compact discs (CDs) by direct mail. If you mail just to prospects who have recently bought a CD player (and filled in the guarantee card) and also have lots of disposable income (they buy shares), they are much more likely to buy. So, by comparing lists of guarantee holders and registered shareholders, and extracting those people who appear on both, you can make up a mailing list of prospects from which you can expect a much higher response rate.

Direct mail organizations can dramatically improve their response rates by mailing only to subsets of list entries which conform to certain defined requirements. There are companies which buy lists from all sorts of different sources and then sell their services to other companies for credit checking and marketing purposes.

For instance, one such company, CCN Systems in Nottingham, is an offshoot of Great Universal Stores. It holds millions of records – different lists from different sources, which can be cross-referenced, compared and related. Their computer holds a list of every address in the UK plus 30 million financial details and 2.5 million personal profiles. Their sources include government census information, council electoral roles, the Post Office Postal Address File and county court records of bad payers. This mix of socio-economic, demographic and geographic information works so well that CCN Systems is now a multi-million pound company, trading lists with other companies and selling their credit checking and marketing services.

CCN Systems operate to standards which go beyond those required by the Data Protection Act of 1984, but databases of personal details are built and swapped around between companies so frequently now that it is getting difficult to keep track of where details came from originally. The individual is at a distinct disadvantage in any dealings with the big database users. The Data Protection Act was passed in 1984 to safeguard the interests of the individual and guard against the improper use of personal data.

The Act also allows the UK to ratify the Council of Europe Convention on Data Protection. The Convention was agreed to ensure that data can flow freely between all European countries. Our Act therefore plays a role in protecting our international trade.

There are eight internationally agreed principles of data protection which form the basis for the 1984 Act. Data must be registered with the Data Protection Registrar, and personal data must be:

● Obtained fairly and lawfully.
● Only held for lawful registered purposes.
● Only used or disclosed for registered purposes.
● Adequate, relevant and not excessive for registered purposes.
● Accurate and up to date.
● Not kept longer than necessary.
● Made available to data subjects on request.
● Properly protected against loss or disclosure.

The Act applies only to computer-held data and sets only a minimal framework of standards. Also, it is difficult to see how it can be enforced effectively. For instance, you are entitled as an individual data subject to see what information is held about you – if you know who to ask! But, unless it is inaccurate or otherwise in breach of the Act you are not entitled to have it changed or erased, or prevent it being passed on to other data users. Also, you are not entitled to know where the data came from in the first place – which may make it impossible for you to know whether it had been obtained fairly and lawfully.

There are also problems in enforcing data users to comply with the law. Personal data should not be kept longer than necessary, but how long is this? Data elements can be transferred from list to list, so a new list may consist of some elements originally collected long ago. If you overspend your credit card limit as a student, how long will this affect your credit rating? Will this black mark dog you wherever and whenever you need credit for the rest of your life? In fact this is unlikely to happen, as commercial motives and ethical considerations will require data managers to use clean, up-to-date data. The worries still remain, however, and we have yet to find satisfactory answers to these tricky questions.

Looking on the bright side, however, database power can also be used for wholly good and benevolent means. For instance, databases can do for community healthcare what they are now doing for marketing. They can be used to focus the energy of healthcare teams on those individuals in the community who need it most, and at the same time remove a huge administrative burden, making the team more effective and efficient.

A modern general practice may have six to eight doctors serving 15,000 to 25,000 patients. Patient records are still held in the old brown medical record envelope (MRE) in some practices, but they are beginning to be replaced by computer records. Old practices often employed more receptionists than doctors, and the office where they maintained the MRE filing system was often bigger than the patients' waiting room.

The wider use of databases in community healthcare will allow preventive care to be focused more effectively on those specially at risk of suffering from certain diseases. We know, for instance, that some people are more at risk of suffering from coronary heart disease. Men are affected more than women, overweight people more than those of correct weight, people with high blood pressure and cholesterol levels more than those with low values, people who smoke more than those who don't, and people from families where the disease has struck before more than those from families where it hasn't.

By using the same database search techniques used by the direct mailing organizations, doctors and nurses can target those of their patients who are specially at risk, and through counselling and advice reduce the incidence of heart disease in the community. As well as avoiding much human suffering, this preventive approach should help to reduce the number of hospital cases and the costs to the National Health Service of treating the disease.

Computer crime

Computer networks with gateways to the Internet are enmeshing the world in ever more complex patterns. This complexity is opening up opportunities for knowledgeable users to manipulate the systems illegally. If you are to stand a chance of detecting illegal use, you need to know in broad terms how it is done.

Society has been very slow in catching up with computer crime, and until very recently the courts could only use the traditional crime classifications to deal with it. But theft is difficult to prove if stolen copies cannot be found and the original data are intact and trespass is no good for dealing with unauthorized access to a computer system. Thus, until 1990 prosecutors had to use theft of the small amount of electricity used during the unauthorized access as the basis for prosecution. Now, however, the law has changed. The Computer Misuse Act of 1990 makes unauthorized access – or 'hacking' – illegal.

Big money is involved. The amounts lost due to computer crime are estimated at over $1 billion in the USA, and run to hundreds of millions of pounds in the UK, though we will probably never know the true extent because organizations are reluctant even to admit that they have fallen victim, for fear of losing the confidence of their customers.

Unauthorized access

There are three main ways of gaining unauthorized access:

- Wire-tapping methods.
- Trial and error methods.
- Password stealing.

Wire tapping methods

Remote access to a central computer often involves the use of ordinary telephone lines. One way of getting hold of the password of a legitimate user is to tap into the telephone wires, perhaps in the same building before the wires go out under the street.

Masquerading

When a user phones up the central computer, but before the user logs-on, our hacker will switch the line to his own PC where he has written a little program to present a counterfeit screen display inviting the user to enter his or her password. The PC will record the password and then send a simulated error message and break the connection. The unsuspecting user will try again, log-on successfully this time, and not think twice about the minor irregularity experienced during the logging-on.

Later the hacker can log-on using the legitimate user's password saved in his PC.

Piggybacking

In this method the hacker's PC is introduced into the line so that the communications from the legitimate user pass through it before being passed on to the central computer. While the legitimate user is logged-on, messages can be intercepted and modified. For instance files sent from one bank to another could be intercepted and additional credits added to the hacker's account.

Trial and error methods

Search-and-try programs

Hackers often write simple programs to help them log-on to remote computers. A program can be written to automate the logging-on procedure, trying a different password each time. With an auto-dial modem and a search-and-try program a hacker can leave the program running all night and look in the morning to see if any attempts have been successful.

Psychological clues

Hugo Cornwall, author of *The New Hacker's Handbook*, gives a list of passwords that crop up time and time again. They include HELP, TEST, SYSTEM, LOVE, SEX, REMOTE, PHONE and FRED.

People usually choose passwords they will find easy to remember, so if you know something about the user you can often guess a likely password. For instance, have you ever chosen for a password your date of birth, or the name of your spouse or children or the football team you support perhaps? If so, with a little bit of research a determined hacker could very quickly discover these and try them out.

Password stealing

Overlooking

When you enter your password, the characters are not usually echoed on the screen. That would make it too easy; the password would stay on the screen long enough for any passer-by to read. Instead the screen remains blank, but that won't stop a hacker looking over your shoulder and watching which keys you press, especially if you are a one-fingered hunt-and-peck typist.

Scavenging

Some hackers will even go to the trouble of going through the piles of rubbish thrown out by the computer department, looking for discarded code on printouts, system documentation, memos and reports – anything that may be helpful in narrowing the search, such as a particular length or format recommended for the password.

Tampering with data

There are three distinct groups of individuals who may try to get at the data in your system to steal or damage it.

One group, hackers, do it for fun and kudos; the intellectual challenge and accolade from fellow hackers is the only motivation. Hackers often contribute to, or run bulletin boards on the Internet. Hackers' bulletin boards are easy enough to set up with a PC and a modem. The culture can be quite subversive – like in the early days of citizen's band radio – with hackers exchanging dial-up numbers of big systems, passwords and information on how to break in. The manager of a bulletin board is call 'sysop', for obvious reasons.

Another group of potential troublemakers are dissatisfied employees or ex-employees who may break into the central computer for revenge, or to restore a loss they believe they have unfairly suffered. Often they have inside information which makes it easier for them to get in. They may have worked in the computer department, or have knowledge of passwords, and their motivation may be theft or vandalism.

The third group are just plain criminals who happen to know something about computers. They are motivated by personal gain, and may use any of the traditional methods such as fraud, illegal transfer of funds, forgery, ransom demands, espionage, blackmail. The computer versions of these crimes have produced a colourful vocabulary of popular terms.

The salami method

When an accounting system calculates employees' pay cheques, it does so only to the nearest penny: any small fractions of a penny are simply cut off and not paid. The salami method involves writing and inserting a few lines of code to collect all these tiny slices and transfer them to a separate account. The slices are too small for most businesses to notice, but can quickly add up to a considerable amount.

If the organization makes payments through the Banks Automated Clearing System (BACS) the payments could be made automatically to a bank account in a false name by electronic transfer of funds, and then the funds could be withdrawn from any of the bank's hole-in-the-wall machines. The irregular lines of code may never be discovered but, even if they are, there can be no fingerprints to link them to any particular individual. Thus for the perpetrator the risks of being caught are very small.

Time bombs and logic bombs

Again, these are irregular lines of code inserted into a legitimate program, which will be activated automatically at a particular date, or when certain conditions are met. Computer criminals can use them in several different ways.

A computer criminal could insert a logic bomb into the central computer of an organization, which would cause the whole system to 'crash', that is, fail in a comprehensive manner, losing data and corrupting programs so that all the system software would have to be set up and reloaded to get the system running again.

Alternatively, the logic bomb could be designed to display a ransom demand and then cause the program to 'hang', that is, lock up and not respond to any inputs until a particular password is entered to unlock the system again.

Legitimate software writers have been reported to be using logic bombs to make sure they get paid for the work they were contracted to do – but in more subtle ways than crudely demanding payment. The software may be coded to start malfunctioning in a less extreme manner, giving the software writer an opportunity to ask for payment of amounts owing before agreeing to correct the malfunction. This is illegal of course, but if software writers warn clients in the small print of the contract, they may still be within the law, though at present the legal position is unclear.

The Trojan horse

In Greek mythology, the well-defended city of Troy was invaded by deceiving the Trojans into thinking that a large wooden horse left outside the city walls was a gift from the gods. They pulled the horse inside the city and during the night soldiers climbed out and opened the gates. Thus any apparently innocent computer program could contain some extra mischievous lines of code and could be used as a Trojan horse. For instance, you may be tempted to load a computer game on your computer at work. If so, don't. It may not be all that it seems.

Data diddling

This is the simplest form of computer crime. It simply involves changing data or entering incorrect data. Examples might be a student hacking into the college computer system and changing the record of his or her grading or an employee gaining access to the payroll system and giving himself or herself a pay rise. Data diddling is the most common form of computer crime.

Viruses

Just as a program can be written to copy a file from disk into memory for instance, so a program can just as easily be written to copy itself into a free area of memory. Then the two copies will copy themselves to give four copies. The four will become eight, then sixteen and so on. Very soon the whole memory will be filled with copies of a program which has no purpose other than to reproduce itself. At this point the computer will stop, completely disabled.

Any program that can replicate itself automatically is called a virus. A virus can be attached to seemingly innocent programs which act as Trojan horses to carry the virus, or they can contain instructions which allow the virus to be spread through a computer network. Thus they are very infectious and extremely dangerous.

In 1988, a student at Cornell University unleashed a virus into the forerunner of the Internet, Arpanet, the computer network which connected university and Department of Defense research laboratories across the USA. It did damage which cost close on $1 billion to put right, and the student, Robert Morris, was found guilty and sentenced to 400 hours of community service and a fine of $10,000.

Computer security

There can never be a 100 per cent secure system. If enough people are determined to break in, sooner or later someone will find a way. Part of the problem is that the more secure you make a system, the less easy it is for *bona fide* users to use. There has to be a compromise, and the costs of the inevitable breaches must be budgeted for. For instance, a couple of years ago, the credit card organization Visa International, budgeted for a loss of more than £130 million in fraud. However, they said that was acceptable because it represented less than 1 per cent of turnover. In 1995 the UK banks lost £83.3 million from plastic card fraud, some £3.5 million attributable to fraud involved with the UK's 22,000 ATM cash machines.

Computer security depends on a combination of physical barriers, software defences and security procedures.

Barriers, software and procedures

Physical barriers consist of making sure that computers and terminals are locked up and only accessible to legitimate users. It is also important to make sure that disks and tapes are similarly protected. All disks from outside the organization should be regarded as potential sources of infection, and should be checked and, if necessary, disinfected, on a stand-alone 'dirty' machine set aside for the purpose, before being loaded onto the organization's mission-critical networks and machines. The risks are real, and companies regularly go out of business within twelve months of a virus infection if vital files such as outstanding invoices or customer databases are lost.

Networks make physical barriers difficult, because telephone wires cannot be completely protected physically. However, for extremely sensitive telecommunications links, such as those connecting military computers to missile-launching facilities, physical barriers are used. The cable is passed down a pipe containing a pressurized gas. If any attempt is made to break into the pipe, the pressure drop will be detected and trigger an alarm.

Software defences usually depend on passwords and personal identification numbers (PINs) in conjunction with cards and cryptography.

Passwords should be changed regularly. If you are ever responsible for systems security, make sure users choose passwords which are not proper names or real words, preferably a random mixture of letters in upper and lower case, numbers and punctuation marks, to make it difficult for hackers to guess. The danger then, of course, is that legitimate users will forget their numbers or, worse still, write them down in accessible places. Often a satisfactory compromise is to choose an easily remembered word or number, with one or two random characters introduced somewhere in the middle.

Cards and PINs similar to those used with credit cards can be used, and cryptography can be employed to code transmissions across networks in such a way that only the intended user can decode the message. The growth in commercial use of the Internet has led to the development of so-called 'firewalls', which are designed to protect a company's internal networks from infection or intrusion from external networks.

Finally, procedures should be in place to ensure that codes and passwords are changed regularly, and that audits of system performance are regularly carried out. The system should maintain files of all transactions, so that an audit trail can be followed by an auditor to check that no irregular transactions have occurred.

Trends: managing information in the future

There are four trends which we can identify and use to anticipate how managing information may develop in the future:

- Advances in technology.
- Cheaper computers.
- More costly humans.
- Continuing change.

Advances in technology

An argument for putting off buying a new computer is to save on the cost of the purchase. Why? Because the price of a given level of performance drops by about half every two years. This has been true over the last thirty years, and shows every sign of continuing to be true into the future.

It certainly makes it expensive to stay at the leading edge of developments, but if you are prepared to purchase hardware based on two-year-old technology, you can turn the argument around and save money by buying a computer now.

One measure of performance is the amount of storage available in a computer. Take a look at the way main memory and secondary storage in the PC has increased over the years (Figure 6.4). Main memory, you will remember, is the actual computer circuits which hold the software you are using and the files you are working on, so with more main memory you can run more sophisticated programs, and you can process larger files. Secondary storage is any kind of permanent storage. Tape is used for batch processing and archiving, but is no good for on-line, interactive processing which is the trend now. Disks are required for that, so the computer can go straight to a particular file anywhere on the disk, instead of having to start at the beginning and 'fast forward' through all the earlier files.

Another performance measure is the speed with which a computer carries out the fundamental instructions that are the elementary bricks from which all programs are built. These are measured in MIPS, millions of instructions per second, and the speed continues to grow. You notice the difference immediately if you go back to using an old word processor after using a new one: the time it takes to scroll through a long document soon gets your fingers drumming.

Computer peripheral hardware such as printers, secondary storage and screens are all still developing.

● Printers have passed through dot matrix and daisy wheel to laser and ink-jet in the space of twenty years. Prior to that, the old tele-typewriter had reigned supreme for decades. Colour ink-jet printers are now cheap enough for home use.
● In the 1960s secondary storage consisted of stacks of punched cards and punched paper tapes. These soon gave way to magnetic tape and Winchester disks, then floppy disks: originally 8 inch diam-eter, then 5.25 inch and now 3.5 inch. It seems unlikely that magnetic media will be developed much further, but the CD-ROM, compact disk read-only memory, and solid-state devices will prob-ably be developed further. Hard disks first available on PCs in the 1980s had 10 Mb capacity. In 1997 it is common for a home PC to have 2 Gb capacity – a 200-fold increase.
● Screens have only recently been developed beyond the TV tech-nology of the 1960s. Development was stimulated by the arrival of the laptop PC in the mid-1980s, which required a flat screen. Then, in less than ten years, screens advanced from tiny, liquid crystal displays (LCDs) in black and grey, through black and orange plasma discharge displays, to full size, full colour flat screens based on the thin film transistor (TFT) technology launched by IBM and Toshiba in 1993.

Cheaper computers

In 1951, the Univac computer cost $2.5 million. By 1980 it could be duplicated on a single circuit board costing less than $500.

In 1976, one megabyte of RAM main memory cost $170,000. By 1979, it had fallen to $15,000. Now it costs about $30.

In 1960, one megabyte of disk space cost $130. Now it costs less than 50 cents.

Growth in PC Main Memory

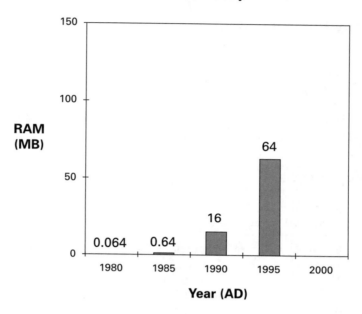

Growth in PC Disk Size

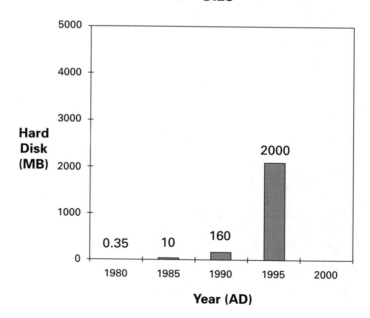

Figure 6.4 *Advances in PC memory and hard disk storage*

On average, over thirty years the cost of a given level of computing power has fallen by about half every two years.

More costly humans

People are becoming more expensive to employ. Standards of living continue to rise, and so too do people's expectations. Someone earning £2000 per annum in 1970 would expect £30,000 in 1996 for the same job. As a result, services are tending to get more expensive in real terms, at a time when many manufactured goods, especially computers, have fallen in price.

Continuing change

Everything seems to indicate that we are in for a period of change which will continue at least for some years to come:

● Throughout the world, political change is sweeping away nationalized industries and reducing state regulation.
● There are few barriers to free trade throughout Europe now, and sterling may one day join a common currency with Europe.
● China, Eastern Europe, Russia and the CIS are developing as huge new markets and opportunities for investment.
● Organizations will be exposed to competition of growing intensity, as markets become increasingly globalized.
● Buyers' markets are likely to prevail, with product prices falling as more and more sectors of world markets become oversupplied. The consumer is firmly in the driving seat, and is unlikely to give it up. Services and products will sell on quality, delivery, variety and price.

Only a major catastrophe of world-wide proportions could halt these trends. Of course it is possible that a political crisis may lead to another world war, a breakdown in international trade, or a world-wide economic depression, but so long as we can avoid global disasters, the trends seem set to continue.

So what are the implications? What should you and your organization do, and what plans should you make to take advantage of these trends? Read them through again, and see if you agree with them. They all point to more intense competition, which will require organizations to:

● Use human resources efficiently.
● Use human resources effectively.

Using human resources efficiently means using them as little as possible for tasks that can be automated. It is efficient to use one man and a JCB digger to shift earth instead of twenty men with picks and shovels. Similarly, we must find ways to automate the handling of all our routine information. Information systems are cheaper, faster and less prone to errors.

Using human resources effectively means using them for the tasks they are good at, and for which computers are quite useless. We need people, not computers, for the creative, imaginative, inquisitive roles that are essential in good design, research and development. We should use people to make value judgements, to develop their inspirational and intuitive abilities to forecast trends and tune in to customer needs. And, above all, we need people to push forward, to motivate, to switch on the computers and keep them running, and to carry the organization forward towards its goals.

For you as a manager somewhere in the middle of your organization, this may sound great in theory; you may agree with these conclusions, but what can you actually do? The way you manage your information is dependent on the total system in which you work. How open are your channels of communication? If your organization is bureaucratic or needs a new management information system there is little you can do about that, apart from lobbying for change, and being ready to play a role when opportunities arise.

The effective and efficient use of humans at work is intimately connected with the way information is managed throughout the organization. This partly depends on computer skills, and knowledge of techniques like the kaizen tools which you can use, but to a much greater extent it depends on more general management developments such as the move towards flatter organizational structures, Japanese management styles, intrapreneuring, empowerment and total quality management. The responsibility for initiating these developments lies at the top of the organization.

Teams throughout the organization must be empowered and motivated to make decisions, and this means, in the words of George Fisher, previously Chief Executive of Motorola and now CEO at Kodak, 'The notion of control has to be thrown in question.' He accepts that he cannot directly control more than a small part of Kodak's operations. His influence, however, lies in his power to encourage strongly a culture of staying close to the customer, and empowering individuals and teams to make their own decisions.

Technology has a big potential role to play in aiding human interaction within and between teams. The new jargon terms are groupware and CSCW, which stands for computer supported co-operative work. In 1990, Japan's Ministry of International Trade and Industry launched an eight-year project aimed at developing CSCW. The Department of Trade and Industry is also promoting CSCW in the UK. With kaizen the Japanese have already shown us how to use teams to cut waste and eliminate quality problems, and that was without using groupware. The race is on: the important global markets of the future will belong to large international teams using

CSCW to research and develop tomorrow's new products and services. Will we learn how to use technology to support our informed and entrusted teams? Or will we use it to command and control individual operators?

To meet the continually rising expectations of our customer, the global citizen, we must learn how best to manage information, which is, in the words of John Sculley, Chief Executive at Apple Computers, the strategic resource of the 1990s.

Competence self-assessment

1   What is the name of the Act of Parliament recently passed to deal with computer crime? Why was the existing criminal law unsatisfactory for dealing with computer crime?

---

2   Describe in three or four lines each of the following: the salami method, the Trojan horse and the logic bomb.

---

3   To what kind of attack from a computer criminal do you think your system at work may be most vulnerable? What defences should be introduced to guard against possible attack? Should you change any of your own practices?

---

4   List some changes in your organization's use of information technology over the last five years. What changes do you anticipate will occur at work in the next five years? What should you personally do in preparation?

---

5   What does CSCW stand for, and how can it be implemented? What two prerequisites are necessary for success?

---

6   Explain in broad terms how EDI works. Who are the main VAN suppliers in the UK? What are the main advantages of EDI? What are the main EDI standards round the world?

---

7   When was the Internet first started? What does TCP/IP mean? What three new developments created the sudden global interest in the Internet? What are its main business-related uses?

---

8   Can you list the eight main provisions of the 1984 Data Protection Act?

---

9 What is the purpose of the 1990 Computer Misuse Act? What are the three main ways of gaining unauthorized access to a computer system?

10 What does CSCW stand for? Give an example of how it could be used in your organization.

References and further reading

Angell, D. and Heslop, B. (1995). *The Internet Business Companion. Growing your Business in the Electronic Age.* Addison-Wesley.

Jacobson, I., Ericsson, M. and Jacobson, A. (1994). *The Object Advantage. Business Process Re-engineering with Object Technology.* Addison-Wesley.

Watterson, K. (1995). *Client/Server Technology for Managers.* Addison-Wesley.

Glossary

ABC analysis – see Pareto analysis.

Alphanumeric characters – all the upper and lower case letters of the alphabet, and the numbers 1 to 10.

ANSI – American National Standards Institute. The American equivalent of the British Standards Institute.

ASCII – American Standard Code for Information Interchange. A set of codes which uses eight bits for each alphanumeric character, plus a range of punctuation marks and simple graphics characters. Originally used for teletypewriters and punched paper tape storage of keystrokes, and now widely used for computer communications.

Binary code – a coding system which uses binary numbers to represent alphabetical letters and decimal numbers.

Binary numbers – a number system like the decimal system, but instead of using ten digits it only uses two: 0 and 1.

Bit – contraction of the term 'binary digit'. It means a single element or figure binary code – a 0 or a 1.

BOM – bill of materials. A structured parts list for a finished assembly. The BOM has the finished assembly at level 0, the main subassemblies at level 1, the parts required for the subassemblies at level 2, the materials required for the parts at level 3, etc. The BOM therefore contains information not only about what materials and parts go into the product, but also information about the order in which the parts are put together during manufacture.

Byte – a set of eight bits. This is the practical minimum number of bits handled by a computer at any one time. In ASCII, one byte is required to represent each of the alphanumeric characters.

CAD – computer-aided design. Special software which allows a computer to be used to prepare designs and drawings. New designs can sometimes produced very quickly by calling up a previous similar design onto the screen and 'editing' it.

CAM – computer-aided manufacture. A catch-all term used to describe any production machinery which runs under computer control.

CIM – computer-integrated manufacture. A comprehensive network of computers and CNC machines which allows a factory to be controlled digitally, without the use of production paperwork, from design all the way through production to delivery.

CNC – computer numerical control. A system of programs and hardware used to control the tool paths, speeds and feed rates of production machinery used for cutting and forming parts made usually of metal.

CSCW – computer supported co-operative work. A generic term covering the team use of teleconferencing, e-mail and any other 'groupware'.

Digital – literally means data which are held in the form of a series of numbers, but usually it is used to imply binary coded data held in electronic or magnetic form.

e-cash – electronic cash. Cash held on a plastic 'smart' card, similar to a credit card, but payments are instantaneous, with no subsequent billing. When the card is empty, it can be re-filled from your bank account.

EDI – electronic data interchange. The exchange of commercial information between customer and supplier in digital form, directly between their respective computers, or via an intermediate third-party computer service.

Electronic commerce – The new name for EDI, but may also cover ordering, invoicing and paying by e-cash over the internet

e-mail – electronic mail, sent through a network from one computer screen to another or many other screens. Almost instantaneous communication, far quicker than snail-mail, the old postal system.

e-zine – an electronic magazine, published only, or primarily, on the World Wide Web.

Firewall – hardware or software installed on an organization's internal network at the gateway to the Internet, to protect it from unauthorized intrusion or virus infection. Named after the firewall installed in early aeroplanes between the cockpit and the engine compartment to protect the pilot from engine fires.

Gantt chart – a horizontal bar chart, with calendar dates across the top, advancing to the right. Down the left side is a list of orders, people, machines or tasks. Thus bars can be drawn in to represent periods of time when orders are being worked on, persons are on holiday, machines are occupied or tasks are being performed. The length of a bar represents its duration and the ends show its start and finish dates.

Groupware – software to encourage co-operation between the members of a group. It usually offers members a common view of the data being worked upon, and depends on communications and database facilities.

Histogram – a diagram in which columns or vertical bars side by side and touching, are used to represent frequencies of various ranges of values of a quantity.

Hypermedia – similar to hypertext, but the top file and its linked files may all be multimedia files. For example you might click on a photo of a bird to hear its song.

Hypertext – A text file which contains highlighted words that act as hot links to other text or files. By clicking on the hot link, the connected text is displayed. For example, you might click on a jargon term to see its glossary definition.

IM – the Institute of Management, the UK professional body for managers, the largest such body in the whole of Europe.

Internet – the network of networks which started as an academic network for scientists in the 1960s, but has created huge interest since it was opened to the public and made more user-friendly. Dubbed the information superhighway by the media, it is often just called the Net by users.

Intranet – the name given to any private network for employees using the Internet hypertext protocol and browsers. Intended primarily for internal users, it can also be accessed through the Internet from outside by authorized users only.

Intrapreneuring – the encouragement of an entrepreneuring spirit amongst managers and employees. Progress through the taking of small risks is encouraged and rewarded.

Inventory – another name for stocks of materials, work in progress and finished goods.

ISDN – integrated systems digital network. This is a communications standard for new networks being set up by British Telecom and Mercury to handle high-speed, real-time digital communication. These networks can also carry voice and moving video, and so are ideally suited for teleconferencing.

Ishikawa diagram – a fishbone diagram for analysing the root causes of some observed effect. Invented by Kaouru Ishikawa, a Japanese professor.

ISP – independent service provider. Someone who controls a mainframe node in the Internet, and offers a dial-up gateway into the Internet for a fee. The fee may also cover a disk allocation for subscribers to prepare their own Web page.

IT – information technology. This term covers all the hardware and software used for storing, processing or communicating information. It includes computers, telephones, satellites, fibre optics, videos, etc.

JIT – just-in-time. A system of production where products are transferred from process to process in transfer batches of one, with almost no buffer stocks between processes. When a process somewhere in the middle of the production routing, finishes its processing and passes an item to the next process downstream, it should receive another item from the process upstream 'just-in-time' to keep it busy. The system depends on tight scheduling, and the highest levels of manufacturing quality.

Kaizen – the Japanese word for continual improvement.

LAN – local area network. A term used to describe the network of communications links connecting up the computers on a single site.

LCD – liquid crystal display. The type of display used in digital watches, with black characters against a greenish-grey background, sometimes backlit. Large LCD displays are commonly used for portable computer screens.

Lead-time – the time that elapses between ordering the manufacture or delivery of something, and subsequently receiving it.

Lorenz curve – this is another name for the Pareto curve. See: Pareto analysis.

MIS – management information system. A network of computers, usually linked to a central large computer and database, for accessing, storing, processing and communicating management information within an organization.

Modem – a contraction of the term 'modulator–demodulator'. It is a piece of gear which translates computer binary signals into sounds for transmitting through the telephone network. When the sounds arrive, the modem at the other end converts the sounds back into binary code which the receiving computer can understand.

MPS – master production schedule. A statement of the total requirements of finished products to be produced week by week for the next six months or so. It is the final result which the production planning department should be aiming to achieve, and is derived from sales forecasts and orders received.

MRP – materials requirement planning. Computer software for working out when parts should be made, and when materials should be ordered. It takes the master production schedule, which is a statement of the weekly requirements of finished goods, and works backwards in time to find out when the parts and raw materials should be scheduled to be delivered.

MRP-2 – manufacturing resource planning. MRP software which has been developed and enhanced to take in the scheduling of all manufacturing resources for a given MPS, not just materials and parts, but also the acquisition of finance, machinery, personnel, etc.

Multimedia – computers and programs which deliver not only text and numbers, but also photographic images, moving video and stereo sound.

Normal curve – a symmetrical bell-shaped curve, which often crops up when the histogram is plotted for a set of figures that tend to cluster around a central or average value.

Objects – modular software entities which also contain data. They model real-life objects such as 'account' and 'customer' and can relate to each other just like the real-life counterparts. They can be used to construct an information system to model the business of the organization. Quality and speed of coding is increased through re-use, and inheritance (the objects 'personal account' and 'savings account' both inherit characteristics from the object 'account'). Object-oriented information systems take between half and one-tenth the time to build, and are easily fine-tuned to the needs of the business

Parallel communications – a system of communications in which the eight bits of a byte travel in parallel down eight parallel wires to arrive simultaneously at their destination. Thus it is eight times as fast as an equivalent serial link.

Pareto analysis – also known as ABC analysis and 80/20 analysis. It is used to sort out the important few items from amongst the less important many other items, and is named after Vilfredo Pareto, an Italian economist who discovered that 20 per cent of the population of a country will typically own 80 per cent of the wealth of that country. The analysis is performed by ranking the individuals in order of descending wealth, then finding the worth of the first 20 per cent.

PERT – project evaluation and review technique. This is a project planning and control method which involves representing all the various component tasks as arrows arranged in their logical order. Some tasks can be carried out in parallel, and some tasks cannot start until other tasks have been completed and so must be chained in sequence. The result is a network, and the longest chain – or critical path – through the network determines the minimum time required for completion of the whole project. The underlying method is also known as critical path analysis.

Project – a project is the work that must be done in order to achieve some future goal. The work is split into tasks to be performed by specified personnel, which are scheduled before the start of the project, to achieve the goal by the due date.

Protocol – a set of rules and procedures to allow computers to communicate. There are many different protocols in use, for instance file transfer protocol (FTP) and transmission control protocol/internet protocol (TCP/IP).

Quality circles – a group of workers who meet outside normal working hours to discuss ways of improving the way in which things are done at work. The groups, also known as quality improvement teams, are paid for their extra efforts and encouraged by management to study and acquire any skills they may need. These groups of up to ten workers are often led by a supervisor, who acts as coach, mentor and adviser.

RAM – random access memory. In theory, this means memory where an item of stored data can be accessed without the need to read through all earlier items to find it, as is the case with serial access media such as magnetic tape. In practice, RAM is now only used to describe the memory circuits of a computer which hold data and programs while the computer is switched on. Each item of data has its own address in memory and can be accessed directly.

R chart – a continuous graph of the range of values found in samples of fixed size taken from the output of a process. If the ranges charted begin to grow, an upward trend will begin to show, indicating that variability is on the increase. This may not affect the average size being produced if the variation causes values to occur both further above and below the average. Without the R chart an increase in variation may thus go undetected.

Revenue – the total income of an organization before any costs are deducted.

ROM – read-only memory. A form of computer memory which cannot be erased or changed, and which is not lost when the computer is switched off or re-set. It is used for instance to hold the small set of coded instructions telling the computer where to look for the operating system when it is first switched on or re-set.

Run chart – a continuous graph for monitoring single samples taken from the output of a process. If there is any drift or gradual change taking place, it will show up as a trend on the graph.

Serial communications – a communications system in which the eight bits of a byte travel in series, one after the other down a single wire. It is a simple system which can use telephone wires for long-distance communications.

Spreadsheet – a computer program which divides the screen up into columns and rows. At the intersection of each column and row is a cell which can contain a value or a formula which the computer will compute. Thus, for instance, a column of figures can be entered, and the total automatically found by entering a formula at the foot of the column. It is also possible to sort figures into order, present the figures in the form of a graph, etc.

Standard deviation – a measure of scatter, or variability in a set of figures. The simplest measure of scatter is the range – calculated by subtracting the smallest value from the largest value – but this is unreliable because it is derived from just two figures. The standard deviation, however, is derived from every figure in the set. The first step in its calculation is to find the deviation, or distance of every figure from the average for the set.

Teleconferencing – users on a network, accessing a central database and communicating with each other in real-time by text messages, and sometimes also by voice and video pictures. The users share a joint view of their work, which may be in the form of text, graphics, scanned images and hand drawings.

Teleworking – using a phone, fax and computer communications to work from home instead of commuting to work every day.

TQM – total quality management. A management philosophy which trains, encourages and empowers everyone in the organization to apply a systematic approach to manage their own work and solve their own problems. Whoever receives the output of your work becomes your 'customer', and exceeding his or her needs should be paramount.

VAN – value added network services. The service of a network provider who does more than just carry messages. It is usually taken to mean EDI services.

Voice-mail – a system for storing voice messages for retrieval by the addressee(s). It works in much the same way as e-mail, and the messages may be stored digitally and reconstituted only when the addressee logs-on to collect mail.

WAN – wide area network. The network of communications links used to connect up computers which are located on several different sites, sometimes on different continents.

WIP – work in progress, or work in process. It consists of partly completed work, such as subassemblies for building into finished goods, and partly machined products.

World Wide Web – the tool known as the Web which allows hypertext access to the Internet, only introduced around 1993, and now by far the most popular choice for business and domestic users. Other tools on the Net include Telnet for remote log-in, and WAIS, the Wide Area Information Service for information retrieval.

$\bar{X}$ chart – a continuous graph of the average values of small samples of fixed size taken from the output of a process. It is at least twenty times more sensitive than the run-chart in detecting small changes in the output.

Appendix – a beginner's guide to the Internet for managers

Internet addresses

The first thing you see on visiting the Internet is the home page of your service provider - a multimedia page of text and graphics. Some of the graphics and some of the text will be clickable hot-links to other pages at the same site, or other sites around the globe. These hyper-text links are the easiest way of 'surfing the net', but if you know the address of a particular site, you can go directly there by pulling down the 'File' menu, selecting 'Open', and typing it in at the dialogue box.

On the World Wide Web, these addresses are known as universal resource locators, or URLs, and they follow a format which reveals the type of site they name. This domain name system is hierarchical, with the most specific name at the left, and the most general domain at the right. For instance, the URL of the Oxford Brookes University site is http://www.brookes.ac.uk Starting from the left:

- http:// – stands for *hypertext transfer protocol*.
- www – stands for World Wide Web.
- brookes – obviously for Brookes University.
- ac – indicates it is an academic institution.
- uk – located in the UK.

If the site is in the USA, the final geographical domain of 'us' may be omitted, as sites were originally assumed to be in the USA unless otherwise stated. Other geographical domains include 'ie' for Ireland and, 'jp' for Japan.

In the penultimate position, eight different types of organizational domain code are common. These are as follows:

- com, or co in the UK – a commercial or industrial organization.
- edu or ac in the UK – an academic or educational institution.
- gov – a non-military government department.
- mil – a military or defence organization.
- org – a non-profit or research organization.
- net – a network operation, or service organization.

Netiquette

The etiquette of the Net originally emerged during the period of its development for non-commercial, mostly academic research users who needed to keep in touch while working at institutions widely scattered across the USA. They were a close-knit group who felt they 'owned' the Net. They valued the resource and felt proprietorally towards it, and would self-police any behaviour they disapproved of, such as wasting of bandwidth and storage space by sending unnecessary or large files. They valued the non-commercial atmosphere, the freedom from censorship and centralized control. However, the astonishing growth of the Internet since 1993 driven by home and commercial users, means that academic users are now a minority, and consequently the netiquette is changing. A battle is being fought between the old school free-thinkers who believe in democracy, freedom of speech and self-policing, and the newer commercial interests who are demanding censorship, regulations and controls.

However, the principles of good communication apply just as much to the Internet as they do in any other situation, and they can be summed up in the words of Professor R. O. Kapp who, many years ago, wrote: 'Consider the needs of your reader.' Business readers generally don't have time to struggle to find the message inside your words, so make your e-mail:

● Brief.
● Simple (no jargon, unless you are sure it will be understood).
● Direct.
● Informative.
● Personalized, that is, tailored to the reader as an individual.

However, we should accept that e-mail is different from other forms of communication, and so there are some extra principles which apply:

● Be informal. E-mail is less formal than a written memo, but more so than a phone call. You don't need to worry so much about typos or spelling, unless you are speaking to a customer you don't know too well. Also, you can usually abbreviate, or dispense with the 'Dear Mrs Simpson', and 'Yours, Edward' conventions. If you are corresponding daily, 'Hi Wal' and 'Ed' would do. For quick-fire hourly exchanges, the message on its own, or signed off with just your first-name initial is enough.
● Keep messages as short as possible. However, be sure your reader won't think you are being curt or abrupt. Take special care if your reader is not expecting your message, or might see it as threatening.
● Don't SHOUT. People sometimes take offence when words are emphasized in upper case. And besides, lower case is ergonomically easier to read, especially on screen.

- Don't automatically broadcast to mailing lists, either inside or especially outside your organization. There are still enough old-school 'netizens' out there for them possibly to 'flame' you, or 'mail-bomb' you, for the crime of 'spamming', that is, sending unsolicited junk e-mail. Flaming is criticizing you or your organization directly and in public on the Internet. Mail-bombing is sending you lots of long, irrelevant files in order to clog up your in-tray.

The emphasis on brevity and efficient use of bandwidth led to the use of abbreviations in e-mail messages. These will probably die out as e-mail software becomes more versatile, but here are a few of the more common ones, just in case you come across them:

- FAQ – frequently asked questions.
- FYI – for your information.
- RTFM – read the frigging manual.
- IMHO – in my humble opinion.

One way of adding an emotional dimension to this text-based world, is to add 'smileys' or 'emoticons', which are icons constructed from keyboard characters. For instance, if you type a colon, followed by hyphen, followed by close bracket, the effect is a smiley face seen from the right-hand side of the page. There are variations on this theme. Using a semi-colon simulates winking. Using an open-bracket simulates frowning, and so on. These devices can be an efficient way of softening what could be seen as an abrupt message.

Some useful business sites to visit

Cyberspace is infinitely flexible. Like stars in the firmament, some Internet sites shine constantly, whereas others emerge and shine brilliantly for a while before dying away. Also, the Internet universe is rapidly expanding – more than doubling in size each year at the time I put this list together in 1996. Inevitably, therefore, changes will have occurred by the time you read it. The list should nevertheless help you get your bearings when you first practise surfing this new, uncharted medium.

The site addresses, or URLs, mostly start with 'http://www.' So, for instance, where you see a URL listed as 'mondex.com', the full address is in fact 'http://www.mondex.com'. A few sites in the list are marked 'Omit 'www'', and these start only with 'http://'.

Shopping malls
buckinghamgate.com
itl.net/barclaysquare
commercepark.com

Electronic cash
mondex.com
cybercash.com
galaxy.einet.net/galaxy.html (Omit 'www.')

Government positions on electronic commerce
europa.eu.int (omit 'www.')
earn.net/EC/bangemann.html
ecrc.ctc.com
dtiinfo1.dti.gov.uk (omit 'www.')
isi.gov.uk
treas.gov
itpolicy.gsa.gov
business.gov

Business sources
bizednet.bris.ac.uk
emap.com/internet
internet-directory.co.uk
clearinghouse.net/

Value added network suppliers
geis.com
ibm.com
att.com
bt.co.uk

Financial information
moneyworld.co.uk
hemscott.co.uk
trustnet.co.uk
updata.co.uk

Webzines
futurenet.co.uk/t3.html
shiftcontrol.com
webreview.com/

Videoconferencing, teleworking and multimedia
cuseeme.com
imaging.co.uk
realaudio.com
trendy.net (omit 'www.')
demon.co.uk/telework

Find or fill a job
recruitnet.guardian.co.uk (omit 'www.')
peoplebank.com

taps.com (omit 'www.')
topjobs.co.uk

Find a book
blackwell.co.uk
amazon.com
books.com/scripts/lib.exe

Find or sell a car
carshop.co.uk

Find a computer
netbuyer.com

Find a person
bigfoot.co.uk

Don't forget to write down or save the URLs of your own favourite sites.

Index